DIFFICULT ⊦

C000143395

DIFFICULT KNITTING

Memoir of a Childhood
Divided Between Two Worlds

Eve Machin

Aesop Publications
Oxford

First edition published by:
AESOP Publications
28a Abberbury Road, Oxford OX4 4ES, UK
www.aesopbooks.com

A catalogue record of this book is
available from the British Library.

First edition 2021

ISBN: 978-1-914938-00-9

CONTENTS

About the author

Eve Machin, my mother, was born in 1915 in Bristol. For the last 30 years of her life she lived in Devizes in Wiltshire where she occupied herself with archaeology and the writing of poetry which was published in *The Green Book*, *Agenda*, *Quaker Monthly*, *Other Poetry*, and elsewhere. She died in 1999. The footnotes and choice of illustrations are mine.

Richard Blaise Machin
Oxford, 2021

BALLET WITH A BLUE SERPENT

Far from the garden
where we whispered among leaves
my serpent
from the dancers on the grass,
on this eternal pavement
ancient wall for shelter
open sky drifting with clouds
my blue robe
your blue scales

in stateliness
my silver hat
steadies my head
my right arm straight
hand holds your tail
my serpent.

Rigid, hierarchic
these steps
are still the dance
the measure
we learnt together.

No haste now
Wildness
would dull your colour
raise your venom
heads would bow away
children shudder.

Calm

to the drums' tap
this our measure
holds the world together.

DIFFICULT KNITTING

1

'A DIFFICULT bit of knitting!' – this was once said to me about my life. I would have liked it better if he had said 'embroidery', which sounds more gracious, but I saw very well what he meant.

The only way to find out whether all the strands that made up my life can be knit together is to begin at the beginning:

I was born in January 1915, at Stoke Bishop near Bristol, in a Georgian house called Druid Stoke. It had been bought with the money that my mother had inherited from my Austrian grandfather, a wealthy Jewish merchant. My mother was vivacious and impulsive, with striking good looks, Russian rather than Jewish; high cheekbones, slanting blue eyes and thick hair with a tinge of auburn.

My father, a fair and handsome public school boy, was high-spirited and passionately fond of riding, hunting and animals in general. The two met when my mother came to his Leicestershire county family as a paying guest, and were attracted by the complete dissimilarity of either to anything that the other had ever met before.

After a hasty entry by my mother into the Lutheran Church, they were married in Vienna.

Shortly before my birth my father, in tears, told my mother that his own mother was what is now called an alcoholic. My mother, who played with dolls until she was sixteen, had romantic and very unclear ideas about life. Ibsen's *Ghosts* taught her to see drunkenness as inevitably hereditary, and she feared giving birth to a fated creature. This fear and the fact that from my birth I was fed by bottle and kept away from her except for short, supervised periods, made her relationship with me unreal and she treated me as a sort of doll.

I did seem outwardly the little doll that she wanted. For my hair was golden, my skin pink and white with dimples on my hands and knees, She got great pleasure from dressing me. As a child she won prizes in little girls' magazines for the dolls' clothes she made. She sewed dresses and made me smocks, one of which, of silk, had a glass bead in every stitch. For outdoors I was dressed in velvets, furs, and beribboned poke bonnets. I looked down at my silk or velvet clothes, my perfect white socks and shoes, with aesthetic satisfaction but they produced a feeling of estrangement and unnatural docility.

My horror of being kissed or cuddled wounded my father whom I thought ugly. I didn't like the harshness of his voice and the rasping of the hairs on his face. He tried hard to teach me to bear teasing and would push down brick towers as soon as I had built them, and sit me on top of cupboards and pretend to go away.

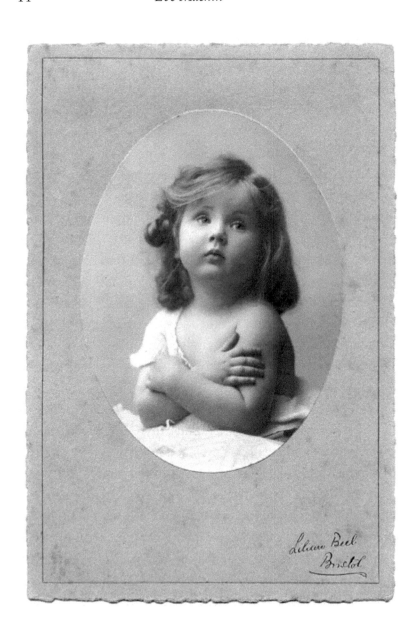

Ours was not a very big household but there were quite a lot of servants. The war had begun and they came and went and were hard to find. This caused my mother to worry perpetually. I reflected her worry as soon as I was old enough to understand it, by running an imaginary registry office under the yew thickets, where I loved playing. This always had just the servant she wanted.

My world seemed both beautiful and terrifying. There was magic in the sunken garden which my parents made of an old tennis court. I gazed at the tight cushions of flowers on its walls. Face to face with them, they seemed to have faces; I saw them as living creatures, silent and moving rarely and gently. They were so much closer than people. Yet they were worlds too and had even smaller creatures living in and amongst them.

I loved trees, with their softly waving branches and fluttering leaves, and the wind, invisible and mystifying, birds bouncing solidly, running on clockwork legs or weaving patterns in the air; and the silent snow.

I was very timid and frightened of everything that moved too suddenly or made a loud noise. Our dogs and even my clockwork toys frightened me. There were fears of haunting things, like the 'wild cat' which I never saw, that came into the house through windows left open at night. In my dreams walked 'Vienna cats' as large and striped as tigers, which slunk about our garden. I sensed when they were about to appear in those dreams, and knew that I had to run and hide under the bedclothes, which brought me back into my real bed. Then once again, I had escaped them.

Vienna was where my grandmother lived – Grossmama – my mother's mother. She sent me pretty postcards and messages about a 'pink dolly' that she kept for me. I sent scribbles and drawings but was not allowed to talk about her to anyone outside the family. It was a secret, for there was a war, and people had been very unkind to my mother, saying bluntly that they wished all her relations were dead.

My English grandfather was driving an ambulance on the Western Front, my uncle was in the trenches, but my father had not been passed A1 because of something wrong with his kneecap. My mother, who couldn't bear the thought of his fighting, persuaded him not to make greater efforts to enlist. He was left in charge of the family business, a leather warehouse in Bristol, and for this he was quite unsuited.

For me the war was 'big dickies': the Bristol fighter aeroplanes which frightened me by their ungainly bumbling across the sky, the ever-changing servants and Uncle Khaki, a friend of my father, who used to visit us. The harsh-sounding name, rough texture and ugly colour of his uniform made me shrink from him. He belonged to a cruel world which I sensed but did not know.

Living with us was Eliza Pidoux, a Swiss woman from Lausanne. She had been my mother's governess since she was eight, and was like a second mother to her. I do not know why she came over to England to be with her at the start of her married life. I grew to love her better than either of my real grandmothers and called her Sasie, which was as near as I could get to 'Tante Eliza'. She was the cause of my learning to speak French at the same time as English. German I would not learn until later.

Sasie, who had been very strict with my mother though she loved her, poured her affection on me. I used to sit up in bed in the room I shared with her and watch her dress. She did not let me see her naked, but I watched her lace up her corset, put on a linen bodice, lace trimmed knickers and grey stockings. What fascinated me most was watching her do her hair. She brushed it over two pads called mice, which indeed they looked like. These gave it a lift over her forehead and then, reinforced by an artificial pony-tail, it was pinned up as a bun at the back. She must have been near sixty at that time: a tall, upright woman with kind, searching blue eyes and a mouth thin with will and endurance. On the mantlepiece were photos of her family which I suffused with the love that I felt for her, and coloured postcards of Swiss lakes and mountains. These seemed pictures of paradise, full of certainty and safety.

My father mismanaged the business so badly that when I was somewhere between three and four we let Druid Stoke and rented a house in Henrietta Street in Bath.

This short period, which must have been somewhat under a year, lies in my memory as a vignette filled with beauty and tranquillity. A slightly sinister note accentuated rather than marred this delightful time – the cry of the rag-and-bone man, incomprehensible and harsh, as he passed through Henrietta Street every morning before I got up. He had a sack over his shoulder and Sasie, with whom I shared a ground floor bedroom, used to say sometimes that if I wasn't good she would give me to him. I hid under the bedclothes when I heard him coming, but didn't really believe her.

The beauty of the squares and crescents and the delicate curve of the streets gave me great pleasure, and the nearby parks, Henrietta Park and Sydney Gardens, had an almost dream-like fascination, with their temples, steps, balustrades and sudden vistas of canal and bridge. The flowers, trees and grass were rare and precious.

My English grandfather stayed with us during this time. He played with me and took me for walks. When we walked down to Henrietta Park the Pink Dolly that Grossmama had waiting for me in Vienna, materialised between us. I wonder what people thought when they saw an elderly gentleman and a little girl solemnly walking, their hands holding the hands of an invisible being between them as they talked to someone who wasn't there.

My grandfather had been rather handsome in his prime and like my father had a way with women and couldn't resist them. He was balding, a great sorrow to him, and he was always ready to try any advertised cure, from raw carrot juice to strange chemicals in bottles. He would bend down so that his head was at my level and ask me if his hair was growing thicker.

Like my father, he was a great tease and I used to get my own back my saying 'no', though if he had been nice to me I was encouraging. Unlike my father, his teasing was always kind. He used to take me out shopping and one day he sent me alone into a chemist: I waited, my head just above the counter.

'What would you like, little girl?'

I held out my coin. 'A pennyworth of good behaviour,' I asked, as he had told me.

'Is it for you?' asked the lady behind the counter.

'No, for Grandad.'

Everyone in the shop was delighted and laughed at Grandad who was standing in the doorway watching. I remained solemn and couldn't understand what the fuss was about.

In Bath my great fascination with the shops was first nourished. There had been a little one in Westbury-on-Trym where my Nanny had sometimes taken me on our daily walks. It had sweets in jars, glossy postcards with photos of romantic girls surrounded by flowers, pencils, rubbers and small toys. The assortment was interesting and everything was cheap: I once bought a moneybox like a little blue letterbox for myself and a rubber the size of a matchbox for my father at Christmas. This lasted for years and was never actually used up.

The shops in Bath were a different matter altogether. They were little worlds that I entered, each with its compelling and distinctive smell and richness of shape and colour. The vegetable shops had earthy potatoes and carrots, keen sharp apples and scented oranges. Each kind of fruit or vegetable was in a heap or pile which seemed to intensify its design and colour. The butcher had his blue and white striped apron, sand-like sawdust covered the floor and the meat was richly red and yellow-white, patterned and formed in lines and curves.

I watched the deftness with which he chopped and sliced. I must have known that this meat had once been animals but it was pure spectacle that held me. Nor did I ever think of shops as places from which to beg presents. I asked only to be allowed to gaze at the red and silver tinselled Christmas displays of crackers, sweets and cakes, and the splendid toy shop in the arcade, full of miniature farms, villages and apple orchards. They all had an unearthly beauty which I would have been sad to disturb. Houses, trees and flowers from that toy shop did appear among my Christmas and birthday presents and my grandchildren still enjoy them. They are rather battered and faded but bring back the magic of that shop in the lit arcade on dark winter afternoons.

During our winter in Bath I was ill with 'flu, had a very high temperature and was moved upstairs into my parents' bedroom. An open fire crackled and flickered in the dark, cosy room and into it came, immensely vivid because of my fever, the world of Beatrix Potter. In my memory it is as lively and real as the magic of the Bath shops, streets and houses. The *Tailor of Gloucester* and *Johnny Town-Mouse* seemed to be taking place around me – the buildings, rooms, area steps and horse-drawn drays and carriages were so exactly what I saw and heard every day.

The year in Bath passed and we were back in Druid Stoke again. Soon after this, Sasie left us to go back to Grossmama, for the war was over. I felt deeply bereft for I had no way of understanding distances in time and space; each day seemed empty and endless. I cried secretly into my pillow at night. Sasie must have guessed how I would miss her and had told me that when I went back to bed I must put my head under the bedclothes and send her a kiss – she would send me one back. As I did this and heard a kiss answering mine, I tried hard to believe it was really her, but soon had to admit to myself that it was Nanny. I didn't tell anyone that I knew, but went on with my kiss night after night – I must have realised, as I did later after the make-believe of Father Christmas, that it was kindly meant.

Some months later, in the winter, my baby brother was born at a Clifton nursing home. I saw him in a cot covered with muslin with a tall muslin hood like a half tent, over the head end. I put one finger into his tiny purple hand and he clutched it hard. Taking this as a sign that he loved me I stood quite still and rather uncomfortable until it was time to leave.

One hears a lot about children of my generation who were either deeply fond of their nannies, or cruelly used by them. My Nanny seemed neither to love or dislike me or the baby who was my brother. She looked after us, took us for walks and sometimes played with us. I cannot remember her ever being unkind to us, nor any joy I shared with her. She was a plain, sallow young woman who gave us neither hugs nor punishments. It was an adequate, cool relationship – her affections must have been somewhere quite different and I cannot remember when she left. At that time I was a reserved, obedient child. The only thing that I held against her was the way she had of dealing with wasps on the nursery windows by cutting them in half with scissors.

When I was five we moved to Shortwood Lodge, the other side of Bristol, between Pucklechurch and Mangotsfield. Shortwood was a mere hamlet – a few cottages and one small shop with jars of sweets and packets of Gold Flakes and Woodbines in the window. Our house was at the end of a mile-long drive through a wood. From the house was a wide and lovely view, over the scarp to the distant Severn.

Shortwood Lodge, early Victorian, long and well-proportioned, white, with sash windows and a grey slate roof, had large grounds which included fields farmed from a Home Farm and a separate stable block. The country kitchen reminded me of Beatrix Potter and I loved watching milk sloshing around in the churn and butter being patted into wet, cool balls or turned out of a wooden mould with embossed cows and trees on its yellow surface. With us in the house were Nellie and Jenny, maid and cook, close friends who soon became part of the family. They worked for us on and off through the years and I took my first baby to show them when they had retired from service to own and run a boarding house in Brighton.

I ran in and out of the kitchen and round the house and garden, exploring. My tricycle had been brought from Druid Stoke, where I had used it very llttle and only up and down the passages indoors and I was delighted with the idea of riding it on the very steep bit of drive which led up to the stables. I pushed it to the top and then mounted and pedalled. I shot down the hill, my feet whizzing round, for I had never used a brake and didn't know what it was for. I landed on my knees and elbows at the bottom, dripping blood and rather surprised, and padded my way round the house, the blood falling in large red drops onto a new grey stair carpet and the lavender one in my parents' bedroom. I must have looked rather pathetic, for I wasn't scolded and surprisingly, I didn't cry, for I was generally rather bad at bearing pain.

The garden at Shortwood had a fairytale unkemptness; overgrown shrubs and trees, mainly laburnum, which Nellie called Golden Rain, and sweet-smelling lilac crowded and drooping round a sunken tennis court. Untidy paths led under trees to a rose-garden, its beds full of unpruned, overgrown bushes of old-fashioned, sweetly scented roses. I never tired of burying my face in first one and then the other of these. Further paths led to a walled vegetable garden and to a cave-like toolshed excavated into the side of the hill. This had a strange smell of earth and cold stone.

Lessons were arranged for me with a young woman who came daily from one of the villages. She was a small, plain, gentle person. I liked so much what she was offering me that I responded and grew fond of her. I believe she was fond of me too, for she praised me and gave me small prizes. I loved writing carefully in the copperplate copybooks, putting my figures in squares in the arithmetic book, and having history and geography lessons read to me.

I was learning to read from a graduated reader and one day decided to take it down onto the floor, where the doctor had ordered me to rest my back every day after lunch. After reading the part that I had already done during my lessons I found that I could go on, and finished the book. My mother bought the next book and I read straight through that. Then I read my geography and history books and realised that I need never stop reading. So I read passionately on and was deeply influenced by books that were given to me. Elves and fairies came alive in hedges and trees, among apples, cherries and roses. My eyes were opened to birds, butterflies, insects, seeds and all natural things. I watched and studied them with absorption. But it was a story of Jesus that changed my life even more profoundly than any other of my books.

Up till then all I knew of religion was from very occasional church services to which Nanny had taken me, the Lord's Prayer which she had taught me but not explained, and a simple, rather sentimental child's prayer learnt from my mother. Neither of my parents had any personal religion; my Viennese grandfather had called himself an atheist, so my mother had had no religion in her home, and my father had completely shrugged off his public school Anglicanism.

Now I read this book about Jesus. I read it alone and every detail struck home.

After Sasie had left I was a very lonely child. My mother was able to breastfeed my little brother Pat and kissing and cuddling him began to come naturally to her. My father and grandfather were delighted to have a boy, and made a great fuss of him. He was indeed a sweet boy. My intelligence, sharpened by my lessons and reading, often became very inconvenient to my parents. I answered them back and refused to say anything I didn't really feel. An alien creature, I was sent for long hours to play in the garden and often punished severely because of their misunderstanding of my rather literal way of thinking. At this time the Vienna Cats changed into the leopards and tigers about which I read in my books and I had constant nightmares.

Jesus, a man who was kind to every sort of person and loved children, brought a great hope to my heart. His execution appalled me but a last chapter promised his second coming, so I began to watch the sky not only as before, to see if I could notice the world really turning round, but to look for changes which would be followed by the last trump. Vivid sunsets seemed full of promise. I knew about death and so apart from my longing to meet Jesus, I found great comfort in the thought that the end of the world could well come before Sasie or Mummy or Daddy or Pat had to die.

Nellie, with whom I shared my interest in Jesus, was a Roman Catholic and sometimes took me up to her attic bedroom to show me her brightly coloured pictures and statues, and told me about the saints. I became rather worried; if I should ever succeed in being really good, how would the Pope know? Lovely though it would be, I didn't think that I would ever have very much chance of being a saint. I copied Jesus and preached to imaginary multitudes gathered on the sunken tennis court. Nellie took me to a Catholic church and using a tree stump as an altar on which I had a yellow stuffed duck as the Holy Ghost, and a little silver bell, which I rang, I held services. As time passed I began to think that the Last Judgement was a very long time coming.

I didn't often see people from the world beyond the drive though there were a few children from 'big houses' with whom I exchanged visits, and I was sometimes invited to a party. These introduced me to conjuring, fireworks and Punch and Judy, all of which, in their separate ways seemed slightly sinister. Any child who could join me in my imagination, I loved. A nice boy called Tim allowed me to play his game of Peter Pan. He had made himself a wooden sword for his role as Peter and generously gave in to my pleading and made me one too – though Wendy did not really need one.

The road which passed the far end of our long drive was very boring. I knew it from walks with Nanny and later with my mother, pushing Pat in the pram. There were fields on either side, full of mud in the winter but with grass, hay or crops in the other seasons. In the gardens of the few cottages which we passed, I could enjoy an antic of my beloved familiar, the wind, as he blew up clothes hung out to dry and made them jig and flap in a multicoloured dance. I also knew the road from my daily rides on Sweep, the pony. My father was a dashing horseman and kept hunters. It was our groom, known in the village as a wife and child beater, who took me out riding. He was rough with horses too and had made the pony nervous, so that it shied at everything and threw me regularly onto the tarmac. The groom's pale and thin little sons appeared in our grounds sometimes and as I had been told about their sad life, they were little spectres of the cruelty which, I was learning quickly, the world barely hid amongst its beauty.

2

AS THE WAR was over at last, my Austrian family were no longer separated from us by a hatred of which I had read an echo in the instructions of a game I was given: 'Buy our games and help beat the Huns.' The Huns I knew were Germans: my grandmother whom I had not yet met, and my dear Aunt Mitzi, whom I had, spoke German. How dare they write like that about the relations I loved! I was filled with a great comforting and righteous fury at impersonal human hate.

When I was told that my Austrian aunt was going to come and stay with us I was so excited that I couldn't sleep. Auntie Mitzi was a thin, dark, brown-skinned woman with a long, sensitive face and sad hazel eyes. She spoke English with a soft Austrian accent and spent a lot of time with me. I showed her my secret places in the garden, and she listened long and seriously to all I had to tell her. I also read her fortune from flowers and told her that she was neither very happy nor very miserable. Perhaps like other oracles before me, I was hedging my bets but I don't think so. I was right and this strengthened the growing bond between us. The little presents she brought with her showed me for the first time unfailing Viennese taste. There were baskets and plates of toy foods, and minute market stalls and booths piled with pastries, flowers and fruit.

Shortly after my aunt's visit I was taken on my first visit to my Austrian grandmother. My father stayed behind with Pat, and his brother, my Uncle Joe, escorted my mother and myself through a Europe just recovering from war. This was the first of so many journeys to Vienna and I find it difficult to separate them in my memory. On the channel crossing my mother, a desperately bad sailor, forced me to sit still and eat dry biscuits. Time proved me to be a good sailor, but on those early crossings I sat still and did what I was told. The roar of the ship's siren filled me with terror and seemed to dissolve me in its fierce sound. For many years I would cram my fingers into my ears when land was sighted.

Then came the climb into the train and a long journey through the night. In the dusk I saw fairies on bicycles and two overpowering, awesome memories still come to me in dreams. The one is of an immensely tall cathedral, towering into the night sky. It seemed to be wavering as I stood gazing up at it, and threatening to crumble down upon me and annihilate me. The other was a mountain. We had got out of the train at a frontier and before us was that mountain, vast and unearthly, upsetting all my ideas of space and height.

My first memory of Vienna is being tucked into a large bed in my grandmother's flat. It had quite different bedding from that I was used to: two huge soft pillows with a small, hard one on top of them, a quilt with a sheet buttoned round it, and instead of an eiderdown, another great pillow, filled with down. Many people were standing round me, all gazing at me with interest and affection. There was my grandmother, Aunt Mitzi and her husband Uncle Alfred and their two children, my cousins Willy and Lilly, who were then fifteen and twelve.

There, also, was the Pink Dolly, nearly as large as me, with long brown curls, a pretty face, an elegant pink beribboned dress and straw hat. She had white socks and leather shoes on her feet. With her were three smaller dolls, pretty little triplets, two girls and a boy. We called the pink dolly Louise after my grandmother and she remained for me and after me for my daughter, a precious possession, to dress and undress, but too out-of-scale with other dolls to play with properly. The triplets were loved and played with for many years. I was also given a doll's nursery, complete with everything, even a work bag which contained minute cotton reels and scissors. Like the toys which Aunt Mitzi had brought me in England, they surpassed in style and elegance everything that I had owned before and were a foretaste of the great joy I would find in Vienna itself.

I cannot remember very much about my grandmother from this, the first time that we met. She looked like a grandmother, as they did in those days. Her skirts were long and dark and she wore buttoned black boots. Like my mother, she did not hug or kiss me, and as her English was very limited, she couldn't talk to me as she did later on, when I had learnt German.

My cousins, particularly Lilly, made a fuss of me, and she has since told me that I was very confiding and chattered to them all the time.

I remember walking in the Prater[1] – not the amusement part of it, so well known for its great wheel – but there were ponds and grass and avenues of trees. I told Lilly about fairies and picked up specks of soil which I said were fairies – so small that we couldn't see them properly. When we got home I made a little room for them in a box and kept them by my bed. One morning I found a fairy doll in the box. I continued the game for Lilly's sake, but for me it was spoilt – the crumbs of earth had really been fairies.

Back in England, life became sad. I did not know that because of my father's bad management the family business was leaking more and more money. Nanny left and my mother was unused to looking after children on her own. My hair was cut short and I was overfed – no longer the little doll with golden curls. I was sent out into the garden for longer and longer spells to play alone and was not allowed into the house until I was called. In between the bright consolations of my imagination which somehow did not come to me as readily as they had done before, and the hours spent reading, there were many lonely, empty spaces.

At this time I made two friends of my own age: a small colliery was beyond the boundary of our estate and in a cottage in a garden which I could reach through our fields, lived a collier with his wife and two daughters,

---

[1] The famous Vienna fairground.

Ellen and Rene. I didn't see them very often, but once in a while I was allowed to go to tea with them. I felt enclosed and safe with this loving family, as we sat round their kitchen table eating doorstep bread and dripping and drinking tea poured from a homely brown pot. They were allowed a wonderful amount of freedom – we made houses with the furniture in their little-used front room and cut up mushrooms for a pretend meal at a wooden table in the garden.

One day, when I was wandering round our garden, I found my mother crying in the shadow of a tree by the rose beds. I had never seen a grown person in tears and stared at her in disbelief. She told me that we hadn't any money and that we would have to sell Shortwood. I stood quite still, listening to her and feeling very sad.

My last memories of Shortwood are of the hall stripped of carpets, the furniture piled up and Nellie sitting on the stairs with Pat on her knees, singing 'Keep the home fires burning'. I stood in the shadows in frozen grief.

What a good friend Nellie had been to us during the years at Shortwood. She cuddled and comforted Pat and was the only grown-up who ever played with me at that time. She would sit at the piano and sing traditional songs with us. When most friends of our own class dropped out of our life when we left England, Nellie and Jeannie sent us cards and Christmas presents and kept up with us until we returned to England again years later.

For my mother had decided that since we no longer had enough money to find somewhere else to live in England, she would take us to live in Vienna with Aunt Mitzi and Uncle Alfred. Her guardians had not approved of her marriage and had refused to allow her fortune to be sent to England. At the outbreak of war it was impounded by the Austrian government. My father had no money of his own and after taking us to Vienna returned to England to find work. Worry had already begun to turn him to drink. We spent our last night in a hotel near the Bristol Zoo. The lions roared in the darkness and at breakfast I was very impressed by the large choice of food. Soon we were in the train, Pat and I looking very smart in grey tailor-made coats and hats trimmed with dark velvet. Nellie and Jean were on the platform waving and wiping away their tears. I waved, stony with grief and dry eyed.

Uncle Alfred was an architect and the four-storey house in which he lived had been designed by him. It was divided into large, comfortable flats. My grandmother was on the second floor and with her was Sasie who had now come to join her; Uncle Alfred and his family were on the third and fourth floors, which were joined by a staircase inside. The first floor, mysteriously, was the Persian Embassy. I cannot remember ever seeing the door open. The building was in the Secession style. There was a lift, which intrigued Pat and myself. Children were not allowed to use it alone, so rides in it seemed slightly dangerous. On the ground floor lived a porter with a walrus moustache which made him appear rather like

Albert Schweizer; he would come from behind his door
when we walked in off the street, seize my mother's hand
and then open the lift with a flourish. In Vienna, I
discovered, men kissed ladies' hands– or pretended to.

The fourth floor in Uncle Alfred's flat held the
servants' bedrooms, a large room with a ping-pong table
and a guest flat. This flat was given over to us. It had a
sitting room with an alcove which held our beds, and its
own bathroom. Our window looked over a big courtyard
where, on a lot of little service balconies one above the
other, you could see maids beating rugs with cane carpet-
beaters, hanging clothes and bedding out to air, and
watering flowers. The house was in the Jaurèsgasse,
previously the Richard Gasse, later when socialism lost
popularity the Lustig-Prean Gasse, but on the latest map
of Vienna I was happy to notice that it was once more the
Jaurèsgasse. This street, at the corner of the Reisner
Strasse just before it meets the Rennweg, is stately and
held several embassies including the British one, and two
churches. The English church was rather sombre and in a
small garden of dark trees, the Russian church which we
could see from many of our windows was a large cluster
of domes and minarets with the oriental colours of a
peacock.

Pat and I were handed over to Willy and Lilly's
governess for most of the day. She was a kind, gaunt,
sentimental German woman called Fräulein Rummel, but
known to the family as Gecki. An orderly life began for
us. We played in the morning in Willy and Lilly's rooms

and went for walks in one of the many parks in the afternoon.

I had brought none of my toys from England with me, except for Louise who I myself carried on the long journey. In Vienna I found some of my mother's dolls with the many old-fashioned clothes she had made for them. I was also allowed to play with Lilly's toys. She had a series of dolls' rooms furnished and fitted in the greatest detail, down to telephones and lavatory rolls. There was also a small room-like closet arranged for her larger dolls as a dolls' bedsitting room. I shared a toy shop with Pat which had little white drawers with sugar, currants, rice and other kinds of groceries that we weighed out on small scales and wrapped in paper bags.

To be allowed to play with these and so many other wonderful toys was like a dream, but for years I had recurring, happier dreams in sleep, when I would find myself back in the nursery in Shortwood before my open toy cupboard, reunited with all my beloved toys. When, years later, this dream came partially true, many of them had been ruined by mice and damp and I was too old to care.

It was important that I should go to school as soon as possible and daily German lessons were arranged for me. A kind scholarly old gentleman came to teach me. To encourage me Grossmama gave me my first pencil case. It was leather with a pen, pencil and a metal cylinder to hold nibs fitted into it. She also made me the first of a series of ten pen wipers, by stitching together several small rounds of black material and sewing them to a large black bead in the centre.

Pat was left to pick up German at his own pace and refused to venture a word until he could put together a small sentence: 'Ein Leut geht auf ein Häus,' he said, and demonstrated it with a match and a matchbox.

After I had learnt German for a month I could write and read in Gothic script and talk fairly well. With Sasie I spoke, wrote and read French and was ready to go to school.

The school that had been chosen for me was called Hanausek and it was in the medieval centre of the town, where the houses crowded round St Stephen's cathedral, and occupied a large first floor.

The Head Mistress was a stern, upright woman of middle age, who looked and behaved more like a Prussian than an Austrian. The Second Mistress was brisk, friendly and gentle. My father, still with us when I first started at Hanausek, took me on the twenty minute walk to school, through avenues and the Stadtpark. Then we crossed the Ring[2] and reached the threshold. Always I started crying. My father could not face walking up the stairs to the school door with a crying child so he stood at the bottom and urged me on, as sobbing and dragging my steps I climbed towards the ordeal of strange surroundings and children who laughed at me.

---

[2] The ring road round the inner city of Vienna.

The kind Second Mistress was there to receive me. She promised me one of the pretty little cards we were given for good work, the first time that I should arrive without crying. They were about the size of cigarette cards and had scenes on them, or pictures of animals, and eventually I collected quite a pack of them. We used to gather round and show them to each other, and say what each one had been given to us for. I was very sheepish that one of mine was for not crying, and had to be very skilful at hiding this without actually lying.

It took some time before my German was free enough of accent for me to be accepted as one of the crowd of children. I did not bear them any ill-will for their teasing; I suppose I realised that it was not really personal or malicious. At mid-morning break we were not allowed to talk until we had eaten the food we had brought with us. I generally had a large roll, heavily buttered, with great slices of delicious sausage on it. As school started at eight I was quite hungry but I wasn't used to such an amount. We had the same rule at lunchtime. The food, the white tablecloth, the silver cutlery, big for my small hands, and the stiff white napkin, which I had to tuck into my neckline overwhelmed me. Not so very many children stayed for lunch and when we had finished we played 'party' games.

There were three other English girls at Hanausek, sisters, and one day during the game of cat-and-mouse, the eldest of the three, a pretty, dark-haired girl much older than I was, drew me to stand in front of her and bent down and kissed the top of my head. I loved her instantly and although I seldom spoke to her again, the school was transformed by her presence.

After that first term my family decided that it was too tiring for me to stay at school for the whole day, but the relief from strain that I might have felt was not to be, for a double remove was arranged for me. This took me into the form of a mistress who had been kind to Lilly. Sadly, she had not recovered from anti-English feelings left by the war and did not at all like the little English girl who appeared before her, sitting in the front row. She was very strict with me, seldom praised me and pulled back my hair, which had been allowed to grow again and fell softly around my face and tied it roughly behind my ears with string.

I was dressed from top to toe as the Viennese girl I was rapidly becoming, in Lilly's outgrown clothes – navy concertina-pleated skirts, sailor blouses or dark jumpers, ribbed stockings and laced boots. I wore a black, long-sleeved pinafore, buttoned at the back, with a large collar trimmed with bands of black velvet.

We worked almost unbelievably hard and except for one writing lesson a week when we practised the script I had learnt in England, everything was written in Gothic. We kept a journal in which we had to enter, to dictation, all that we did – lessons, outings, rehearsals, and the dictation was far too fast for me to take without strain. French was very advanced for our age, and Sasie gave me lessons in the evening, which helped me to keep up. I never again had to work so hard until, at eighteen, I had only three months to be coached up to the standard of an Oxford scholarship.

In spite of all this hard work, there were many things to enjoy at Hanausek. We had lovely visits to castles and churches and the beautiful country round Vienna, and I soon began to make friends amongst the children. My purple and brown leather stamped album reminds me of many of them: Kurt Bauer, a neat and sensitive little boy with short curly hair, Regina Schogorodsky, Russian, rather heavy, with a dark, sleek, fringed bob, Elisabeth Gassauer, fair and lively, Herbet Dollinger who used to ask me to be his partner on walks and tell me long, sad tales about his bullying father, Hansi Frost and Gertie Steiner, inseparable friends, who admitted me into their friendship and asked me to tea.

It didn't take me long to discover that Vienna was a city of music. When I was still quite new to Hanausek, I was one of four children chosen to dance a minuet in a Schubert festival. I wore a long white Broderie Anglaise dress and my partner had blue silk kneebreeches and tailed coat. Even the folksongs we sang were by Mozart, Haydn, Schubert and Brahms. Beautiful music was whistled in the street and poured out of windows on hot summer afternoons.

Soon there was nothing to distinguish me from other Viennese children except my English colouring and, inside me, an indefinable haunting homesickness for Shortwood and Druid Stoke. There was a very sentimental German poem about a little violet which was always being uprooted and planted somewhere else, and whenever I read it I shed uncontrollable tears. Once a month I would sit at a table trying to write a letter to my father and as I gazed out of the window at the clouds, the rooftops and the cupolas of the Russian church, he seemed so far away that I couldn't find the words to send to him. My letters were short and stilted, for there was too much about my life that he wouldn't understand.

The furnishings of this new life fascinated me, so different were they from the things which I had left behind in England. There was the food; every lunch began with soup, which I had always loved and had had far too seldom in my English nursery life. We had compote on side plates as an alternative to salad; meat was most often boiled, but made interesting by a great variety of sauces and herbs.

Nowadays there seems to be a delicatessen shop in most English towns, but they are pale shadows of the ones into which I was taken by Sasie or Gecki, to choose something for our supper, which Pat and I had up in our sitting-room. There were countless sausages for slicing, boiling and frying, all smelling and tasting wonderful. We had slices on the breakfast table too, to put on the lovely crisp rolls and croissants. These were sometimes sprinkled with salt or poppy-seed. I was eager to experiment with new flavours but now and again the memories of English food would stir in me and I would long for a fried English sausage, which I could not have, but when Pat had whooping cough and I stayed in the second floor flat with Sasie and Grossmama, Sasie used to fry me some bacon as a special treat.

The puddings were influenced by Czech cooking and often substantial, with apricots, black preserved plums or apples. For special occasions, luscious Viennese Torten appeared. These and the elaborate ice-cream concoctions were all home-made and none of the ingredients were artificial. It was lucky that in spite of my keen enjoyment of this food I showed no signs of getting fat. Perhaps my helpings were more carefully controlled than I remember. Nearly all the shops were full of delights. Confectioners, into which Gecki would sometimes take us on our afternoon walks, had delicately coloured imaginative sweets, different from the wholesome, simple ones I remembered from England. There were two kinds that we enjoyed particularly: little chocolate disks sprinkled with hundreds-and-thousands and soft coloured, glass-like segments of cylinders which had small flowers and fruit right through them – a fairy version of English seaside rock.

I discovered a special pleasure in stationers' shops, where Grossmama took me to buy all the things I needed for school. There were drawers full of different kinds of pencils – and not only pencils, but special protecting guards for their points; endless varieties of rubbers, penholders, nibs, notebooks and exercise books, paper for covering text books, and sheets and books of shiny coloured paper for cutting out pictures and shapes. We had to keep our exercise books covered too, and I longed for the kind of cover which had a transparent window in front. Paints and paintboxes were entirely different from English ones. The colours came in button-like disks and the boxes were elaborate with layers of pallets for paints which had hollows to hold the paints, and compartments for brushes, for pans for mixing colours and for Indian ink. There was always something that I longed for in these shops when my schoolmates showed off new kinds of notebooks, pencil guards or other proud possessions, and mostly my smaller wishes were granted sooner or later as rewards for good marks or good reports.

The large toyshop in the Kärntnerstrasse rivalled the one in Bath Arcade. Here were Louise's fellows in all sizes and all, it seemed, with real hair and an enormously varied wardrobe. There was furniture for house and garden to fit them all, down to complete bathroom sets with bath, basin, bidet and lavatory, and drawers of spare dresses, shoes and socks. There must have been good toys for boys too, and certainly some fine rolling-stock and soldiers came Pat's way from time to time, but my eyes were only for the world of dolls.

I did not enjoy drapers and clothes shops. My mother would search unwearyingly for some stuff or ribbon for dressmaking and one day, when she was, for some reason, in charge of us, she dragged us over the ice-covered Viennese cobbles for hours, looking for a material then in high fashion, called Kascha – if that is how it was spelt. 'Kascha! Kascha! Kascha!' we mouthed at each other behind her back, with grimaces of revolt and boredom. When eventually she tracked it down, it was a dreary oatmeal colour, and rather coarse.

Vienna and its surrounding villages were full of legends. I learnt some of these at school and others I read for myself in the little paper-backed books edited specially for children, which as a great treat I was sometimes allowed to buy. Once, when I had an especially good report, Grossmama gave me a blue and gold bound book of Grimms' fairytales. This had, as well as the well known stories, many lesser known folktales which are seldom translated. They were illustrated by small woodcuts in which Death, the skeleton with the scythe, was often shown. So I became familiar with medieval Death, who danced on church walls and seized people unexpectedly or led them away gently at the end of their lives.

I knew the exact spot where a water nymph might appear in the Danube – a sort of local Lorelei, who could draw young men into the grey waters. Shudderingly, I passed the courtyard where a basilisk had once lived. There was its statue: a dragon-like bird with a horrible expression that could turn anyone to stone. Right in the middle of the fashionable shopping streets of the Inner Town, on the corner of a house, protected by a grill, was a mysterious tree stump completely covered in nails. It was the result of a pact made with the Devil by an apprentice. Then the iron cross where a sad maiden had sat spinning, waiting for her lover who had never appeared back from the Crusades. There were so many haunted streets, and graves and skeletons in the dark vaults of St Stephen's.

There was another kind of skeleton which caused me a frisson of horror: in the great glass hall of the Natural History Museum stood a vast skeleton of a brontosaurus. It didn't have the mesmeric power of the basilisk, but was the denizen of such a strange unfathomable yet real world, that I felt my own world fading, and trembling beneath my feet.

In contrast to the dark, mysterious Gothic, was the bright, playful and heavenly Baroque. Churches, with their white and gold, their clouds and azure sky, with God, Jesus and saints and angels looking down at me from great heights seemed to be offering a foretaste of heaven. All here was light and secure. My friends were allowed to behave in a manner worthy of those palaces of God; they crossed themselves solemnly with Holy Water and made deep curtseys to the altar. I wanted to do the same myself, but sadly, although I had been taught how to cross myself at school, I knew that the churches were not mine and felt sad. My church was in England and nothing like these.

The parks were mine as much as any other children's. The Belvedere (quite near to where we lived), the Schwarzenburg Garden, the Stadtpark, the Botanical Garden, the Modena Park and sometimes, rarely, Schönbrunn.

We went with Gecki to the Belvedere on so many fine afternoons when the weather was mild or warm. The

Belvedere itself consisted of two palaces spread out in baroque splendour at the summit of a steeply rising slope. Its park rose over two terraces. There were wide flights of stone steps, large and small stone basins of water and everywhere, even on balustraded portions of roofs and in the centre of stretches of water, statues: rearing horses, naked or draped men and women, cherubs and sphinxes.

The gardens had lawns, topiary and tall trimmed hedges and gravel paths. We entered through a smaller building whose frontage was along the street and once past its ornate iron gates and in the gracious palace grounds, we played like royal children, absorbed in our games and exploratory walks, watched over by our governesses. There was never a crowd and there were no loud noises. Here, with our friends, we played ball, diabolo and skipped. The various balls, smelling beautifully of new rubber, we carried in net bags. Sometimes I brought a doll, or we would wander off to small secluded lawns and play imaginary games which needed no toys.

Here, in the Belvedere, I would often find my special friend, Mausi. She was my favourite companion, a lovely little girl with soft, long brown curls, a sweet oval face and gentle sidelong glance. One day, when I had brought a baby doll, beautifully dressed in a long fur-trimmed white cape, Mausi asked me to let her hold her. I said no. A large tear rolled slowly down her cheek. At once I gave her the doll to hold and never again refused her anything during the endless games we played together.

The Schwarzenburg gardens were less splendid than the Belvedere but made an occasional pleasant change; Schönbrunn was infinitely more so, with its Tivoli, great waters, grottoes and vast expanse of gardens, which even contained a Baroque zoo. The Stadtpark was the municipal garden and had a bandstand and a restaurant where we sometimes drank chocolate or ate ices. There were generally one or two men selling balloons and windmills. The Modena Park was the rather gone-to-seed garden of a very small palace. There was nothing much growing here apart from some rather sparse copses, but it had a little hillock. When snow was on the ground and we dragged our toboggan there over the bumpy pavements, this hillock made a good toboggan run.

In spring and summer we were sometimes taken to the Prater. I was never allowed on the great wheel and would have been too frightened to enjoy the precipitous scenic railway or the ghost train. A roundabout that had little carts drawn by real ponies was just right for us. Lilly kept small green tree frogs in a vivarium through the winter, and every spring we went on an expedition to release them into a large pond in the wild part of the Prater. Near the Prater was the great wide swiftly moving Danube, very impressive and not at all romantic. The scenery here was flat and unspectacular and the river a greyish brown.

There would be family outings to the Vienna Woods or to castles or monasteries. Here the Danube was still not blue, but set in a panorama of small mountains, villages and vineyards. We would eat the bread rolls we had brought with us at simple inns, sitting on wooden benches and drinking milk or lager.

So the months and years passed and I put down many roots and learnt to love Vienna as my home.

3

IT WAS IN VIENNA that I learnt the meaning of the word 'family'. My grandfather had been one of at least twelve children and my Grossmama one of six. My mother had dozens of cousins but they had few children. The fall of the Austro-Hungarian Empire had had its effect: families were beginning to disintegrate and in the city of Freud amongst the very classes from which his patients were drawn, 'affairs' amongst the married and unmarried were common. On the other hand the concept of family was enormously inclusive; no matter whether it were a question of blood relations, relations by marriage, or cousins so distant that no-one could quite account for them, all were included.

Also a kind of feudalism lived on. I remember an almost ragged little old woman who appeared in Grossmama's flat and after kissing her hand, talked to her in an impenetrable Bohemian accent. Then she eyed me up and down with interest – 'Frau Charlie's Tochter!'– and was led off to the kitchen for what was her right – a good cooked meal. I have no idea how she fitted into our complex connections.

The family would appear in ones and twos, or larger groups, at almost any time and we were dressed up and taken by my mother on visits. Most of our relations lived in Vienna but some were still in Czechoslovakia, the Bohemia and Moravia of before the war, in Prague or Brno, which had been the home for several generations of Grossmama's family – the Schwarzes.

At first I felt flattered to be the centre of so much attention, but before very long I became aware that it was not something I had earned in my own right, but by proxy... I watched silently and learned that it was not always those who praised my looks and well-practised curtsey who felt real affection for me, and I distinguished in my mind those I loved from those who irritated me by their falseness and superficiality. I kept this secret even from my mother and Sasie. Pat was more extrovert and clowned at and charmed all alike.

I soon formed a bond with Grossmama. It was affectionate but not like the deep affection I felt for Sasie or the painful love I felt for my mother, who never seemed to return it in any degree that satisfied me. Grossmama Luise and her two sisters next in age, Aunt Toni (Antoinette) and Aunt Jennie (Eugénie), had vivid imaginations and from their earliest days had written poetry, made up plays and games and embroidered their early days with fantasy.

Aunt Toni had had books of children's stories published and Aunt Jennie, a foolish woman, had written reams of sentimental verse and still sent long rhymes full of lilies and roses and birdsong in letters or on birthday cards.

To this family belonged the poet and dramatist Richard Beer-Hofmann who was Grossmama's first cousin and a close friend of Arthur Schnitzler and Hugo von Hofmannsthal. He lived near his cousins in Brno throughout his boyhood and shared their many games which he enriched by his own imaginative and creative gifts. Later he was to become an object of inspiration and veneration to me.

Grossmama used to enjoy talking to me for hours at a time about her childhood and girlhood and I have in my desk a delightful account written by Aunt Toni of the exploits of the three sisters up to the time of first Luise's and then Toni's betrothal and marriage.

My great-grandfather Schwarz was a manufacturer of woollen cloth and the family house was adjacent to the factory. My great-grandmother worked for the business as accountant and it was her mother who ran the household in what her granddaughters considered a far too bossy and critical style. Next in the family, after the three girls, came great-uncle Edmund, the beloved and spoilt only boy. He was a pretty child, with bright eyes and dark, curly hair and was also very intelligent. The spoiling proved disastrous, for in spite of a great love of books he was lazy, and never fulfilled his promise. When the menace of Hitler first began its threat, albeit still from afar, he lost all courage and shot himself.

In the days when I first knew him, Uncle Edmund was a fine large, upright man with white hair and an impeccably white beard. He was very vain about his beard, kept it neatly trimmed and sprayed with eau-de-Cologne and patted it into shape at all times. He would pull me onto his lap and kiss me with soft, moist lips. His hands too were soft and beautifully manicured. My mother was his favourite niece and I in his eyes her natural successor. I didn't like his caresses nor the sentimentality which my mother had loved, but I was good at hiding my feelings and didn't hurt his. Pat, when he first saw him at the age of two, rushed and fetched one of his bibs and held it up to his own chin saying – 'I've got one too!' .

The inventive childhood games of Grossmama and Aunt Toni included hypnotising their canary by rubbing its stomach and then using it as a toy in their dolls' house. In one of their plays Richard, draped in a bedspread was a bride and Luise, handsomely dressed as a man, was the groom. Her wooing was so dramatic and impassioned that the sofa collapsed under her. Weddings and bride 'viewings' were favourite games and quite soon, when Luise was only sixteen the real thing entered their lives.

Toni describes with touching humour first Luise's viewing, betrothal and marriage, and then her own, and one can be astonished at how much excitement, romance and love the girls brought to their arranged marriages.

From the moment that their Mama first tells the two older girls to put on their best clothes *in the middle of the week* and takes them for a walk in the park *in the winter*, to the point where the golden-haired and bearded young man who was to be my grandfather Sigmund, pleased with what he had seen fleetingly in the cold park, pursues the shrinking Luise behind a chest of drawers to press his suit, the romantic excitement mounts day by day.

After a splendid wedding Toni is left in a state of depressed anti-climax. Then dreary ages later, she is taken off to Vienna dressed in Luise's cast-offs. She is shrewd and not at all vain and is pleased to think that she is not deceiving her intended Rudolf, who she notices has kind eyes, into thinking her more elegant by nature than she really is. Hers was a very happy marriage. Luise's Sigmund, though more handsome than small, swarthy

Rudolf, was too serious and matter-of-fact to satisfy passionate and romantic Luise, though their marriage was faithful.

There were two younger children in the Schwarz family: Hilda and Rosa. Hilda, an enchanting child, died at five of meningitis. Rosa died when still a very young wife.

The Schwarzes, unlike the Mandls, grandfather Sigmund's family, were not Jewish to look at and had high cheekbones, broad faces, pink and white complexions and blue eyes. There was a tradition that they had originally come from Russia.

At Luise's wedding Uncle Edmund, a young schoolboy, fell in love with Sigmund's sister Irene, a pretty little bridesmaid. She was fair and delicate featured and when she was a young widow with twin daughters, he married her. He became the most openly adoring husband that I have ever known. He would heap pet names and endearments on my Aunt Irene, kiss her hand and gaze at her with unconcealed sentiment. She in her turn became a very spoilt, arrogant and critical woman.

When I first saw her she was still very beautiful: her hair had changed from fair to a fine white, she had a delicately shaped face and perfect figure and dressed with all possible Viennese chic. I remember her always in pale grey and pastel colours, with perfect and valuable jewellery and diaphanous scarves in exactly the right place. Rather deaf as the result of an illness in her childhood, she had a harsh voice and was cruelly critical of the appearance of others, particularly children. Luckily for me I passed muster on the whole, for my mother, too, had good Viennese taste, but Aunt Irene wasn't past dragging my hair into or out of my face as if I were a puppet and I resented the cruelty with which she criticised her own granddaughter Yvonne, who had sadly inherited the long melancholy face and large nose of her father, instead of taking after her mother Magda, the prettier of Irene's twins. I did not hate, but neither did I love her. Of course I again kept my feelings to myself – to my mother most of her family were well beyond reproach.

After I had been in Vienna for about two years, my grandmother died. She had been in hospital for many weeks and I was not taken to visit her. Like my mother, she was allergic to many drugs and had been given something which had fatally worsened her illness. I was lying on Lilly's sofa with bad earache when Sasie came from the downstairs flat and told me that Grossmama was dead. The tears ran down her face and I envied her. I felt only my own empty despair inside me and could not ease it by crying. I felt that if only I had been able to say goodbye to Grossmama it might have been different.

On the day of the funeral my mother and my Aunt Mitzi were in full mourning and I insisted on putting on my only dark dress, a navy one with a white collar. I was not taken to the funeral but hung around the house sadly and solemnly in my improvised mourning, with

Grossmama's watch, which had been given to me, ticking on my wrist. I knew then the bleak mystery of a death which I had to accept but had not witnessed.

One of the families which I loved without exception was that of my grandfather's sister Ottilie. Aunt Otti Fluss was as different from her sister Irene as was possible. She was tall, dark, with kind brown eyes full of good nature, intelligence and common sense. I cannot remember much about her husband, he seemed to work hard and not do much visiting – a small, neat, quiet man.

Aunt Otti was totally deaf – like Aunt Irene her deafness was due to an illness – measles, or scarlet fever. She had a deep sonorous voice and could lip read perfectly – so perfectly, I found, that it was rash to say anything untoward anywhere in a room when she was there – she only had to *look* and she knew what you were saying. Her children all spoke alike, deeply, slowly and well articulated. They had learnt it from babyhood and my mother remembered how, when they were very young and desperately pleading for some treat, they hopped from one foot to another with impatience but had to control themselves so as to articulate their words slowly and deliberately, to make their mother understand.

There were seven children – five boys and two girls. All of them were great animal lovers and one of the many stories that my mother told me about them was that they had once cherished and fed a family of mice which they had found in the grand piano. Lily, the younger sister had as a grown and married woman rescued and tamed a jackdaw which repaid her by stealing and hiding her wedding ring.

I loved the good-natured, untidy Flusses and particularly 'Aunt Lily'. An enduring affinity has existed between us and at the age of nearly ninety she still writes to me from California, lively letters full of enthusiasm and interest. They were a family with dark, romantic looks. Lily has had a very sad life. Married to the brilliant Italian journalist Italo Zingarelli, she had two little daughters: the eldest, Laetitia was the first baby that I cherished. She died at eight of appendicitis. Italo had left Lily and she lived through this terrible experience alone in a foreign country.

Lolo, who was very like her sister, though taller and fair, married the American concert pianist Ralph Wolfe. I was very impressed when Ralph during stays in Vienna, came and practised for *four hours* on Aunt Mitzi's piano – my own twenty minutes of practising was almost too much for me.

Karl and Robert Fluss I very much loved. They were both, I believe, designers in a ceramics factory. Karl in particular was a delicate and intricate draughtsman and has left me a drawing in my album, in black ink, of gnomes, little animals and twisted roots. He and Robert must have been fond of children for they always seemed happy in our company, or perhaps it was that all the Flusses were children at heart.

We often visited Aunt Toni at her house in that suburb of Vienna called the Cottage. Her small garden with trees, paths and unorganised flowers and shrubs was very unlike an English garden and I loved playing my imaginative games in it. The house was fiercely protected by iron bars, grills and shutters, for Uncle Rudolf had a neurotic fear of burglars. He was also very anxious about Aunt Toni's health, and wouldn't allow her to exert herself or to leave the house except in a carriage. She was, as a result of all this extreme care, fat and moved slowly, but though compelled to be lazy in body, she kept her lively and enquiring mind. She, like my grandmother, wrote and embroidered, and made little dolls in the costumes of Mozart and Haydn, and when her only child, Erich Kahler, Professor of History and Philosophy at Heidelberg, had started as a boy to learn Greek and Latin she learnt with him.

There were many writers and artists among her visiting friends. From this, my first long stay in Vienna, I remember a charming Doctor Willenski, a distant cousin, who was both an artist and a nose and throat specialist. He operated on my tonsils and adenoids in a Viennese nursing home. During his first visit after the operation he praised my courage and asked what I would like as a reward. Pat, in his usual perky way, taking advantage of my inability to answer quickly because of the pain, chipped in: 'A nose-lamp!'. Everyone burst out laughing but the next day 'Uncle' Pepi Willenski appeared with a pretty dolls-house sized glass chandelier complete with bulb and battery.

Uncle Rudolf and Aunt Toni's house was full of books and paintings. They had reason to be frightened of being burgled for when I was older I recognised the work of many impressionist painters – Degas, Monet, Manet, Sisley – and all the paintings were 'good'.

Dr Fürst who was our family doctor was also some kind of relation. Like a doctor in a Russian play he appeared neatly dressed in a dark suit, with highly polished shoes, and carried a black bag. He pressed back my tongue with a spoon and stared into my throat, felt my pulse and listened to my chest with a stethoscope. When he came it nearly always meant a short but happy time in bed resting from school, nice little meals on a tray and reading as much as I could possibly wish.

My Mandl great-grandmother, Grosspapa's mother, had been called Charlotte and four of her granddaughters were named after her – three of them born in the same year. My mother was the eldest of these and so Grossmama had the first choice of abbreviation and chose 'Charlie'. Then came Lolo Fluss and Carla, one of Aunt Irene's twins. The youngest Charlotte was the daughter of Grosspapa's youngest brother, Erich. This man was so much younger than the elder members of his family that when he was born he was already an uncle several times over – this impressed me. He was a handsome man of about the age of Aunt Mitzi and his daughter Lotte Mandl was one of Lilly and Willy's friends.

Mr and Mrs Perutz, who were not relations but had been friends of Uncle Alfred and Aunt Mitzi for many years, lived down the road in a fine flat in the same building as the British Embassy. Mrs Perutz was beautiful, always elegantly and expensively dressed and enjoyed society rather above most of our other relatives and friends. Her husband was a very dark, quiet man who gazed on her beauty and wished for her all that she could desire.

The two older children, Franz and Lotte, were with Willy and Lilly a lot: tearing up and down the street on bicycles, playing table-tennis or just hanging around.

There was also a much younger child, Max, who was a year older than me. I had first seen him at Hanausek where, for a short time, he was in the form above me. He was pale and delicate little boy and I was considered a suitable friend for him. I went with him on sedate outings to the Wienerwald and to his flat for tea. Here several sets of double doors were opened for us to lay out rails, points, stations, turntables and signals for a great railway network. The rolling stock was superb and I remember especially a Red Cross carriage with beds, patients, stretchers and orderlies. As with Mausi, I played with Max in perfect accord.

There were two children whom I hated visiting. They were the daughter and son of one of my mother's distant cousins: this boy and girl cheated and quarrelled and told tales about each other. Although they didn't draw me into their bickering I was always very pleased when it was time to leave. As my mother was not prepared to hurt her cousin's feelings I was made to visit them often. I liked their mother very much and when I met her children again years later they had grown up to be very nice people too.

I cannot leave this account of my Austrian family without describing the festivals which brought us together. Christmas was, as it were, split in two: Father Christmas – Santa Claus – made an early appearance as that child-loving saint, Saint Nicholas, on his festival on December 6th. The shops in Vienna were beautifully decorated for each successive festival and were a wonder and temptation to adults and children alike.

For St Nicholas the colours were white, red and black; the Saint, dressed as a bishop, brought with him as a companion a devil called the Krampus who punished naughty children, while St Nicholas rewarded the good. The little St Nicholases in the sweet shops held staffs of silver or gold and carried a sack of sweets or toys to put in the shoes of deserving children; the Krampuses, fearsomely black with red tongues and red eyes had barrels on their backs full of Karlsbad plums to represent the coal that was put in the shoes of bad children. In their hands they held silver or gold birch-rods.

We put our shoes on the window sill on the eve of December 6th and in the morning found them full of small toys, sweets or plums – never coal as we sometimes feared we might. When we were older and living in Baden outside Vienna, we dressed up as Saint Nicholas and Krampus for the gardener's little boy and after interrogating him sternly to make sure that he didn't deserve coal or a whipping, gave him the presents we had bought for him. Our disguises were fairly roughly homemade so there was little danger that even a three-year-old might have taken us too seriously.

Altogether December and January were months full of blissful anticipation – Pat's birthday was on December 4th and mine on January 17th – so these personal festivals were added to those of Saint Nicholas, Christmas and the New Year. Our birthdays were like pockets in time, our very own days, when we were given our favourite food, allowed to choose our occupations, were visited by aunts, uncles and cousins and reasonably safe from scoldings or punishments.

In the middle of the morning, when the visitors had arrived with their offerings, the 'birthday child', tidied up and smartly dressed came into the drawing-room to gaze at the presents laid out on a small birthday table and be smiled upon and kissed by the assembled relations. The number of presents was not too large and they were carefully and lovingly chosen. Mine would often be some childhood possessions of Grossmama or one of my aunts – a necklace, writing-case, purse or book. My mother, Grossmama and Aunt Toni, so clever with their hands, made doll's clothes, doll's house furniture or little doll's house dolls. I remember also a drawing block, and the type of leather box with straps which Austrian children had, to carry their schoolbooks in. Grossmama and Sasie also added golden sovereigns to save till I was older. Each present was treasured and of special meaning.

At teatime a birthday cake appeared. It was always the same traditional kind, called Kugelhupf. The texture was crumbly, rather like a Madeira cake, it was cooked in a tin which gave it the shape of an English jelly, and was sprinkled with powdery sugar. The candles, one for each year and one 'life-candle', were the size of Christmas tree candles and set in a brightly painted wooden ring around the cake.

The festival of Christmas was celebrated on Christmas Eve. For some weeks beforehand shops were bright with Christmas tree decorations, fragile and lovely, and a market, dedicated to the Christchild, sprang up in one of the squares of the old part of town. Here the stalls were piled with baubles and fruit, sweets and presents of all kinds. Santa Claus was forgotten and it was the Christchild who was to be himself the bringer of gifts.

'Stille Nacht, heilige Nacht' we learnt to sing at school and it is still for me the quintessential Christmas song, holding all quiet, love and harmony.

When we woke on the morning of December 24th we were already almost unbearably excited. The drawing room was barred to us, none of our usual games and occupations seemed to amuse us, and the day crawled along. At six o'clock the magic moment came, when cleaned and tidied we were ushered into the darkened room where the tree twinkled and glittered in silver and gold. The flames of its small candles burnt upwards like a myriad small prayers and were reflected in the bright burden of silver and golden balls, gilt walnuts, glass birds, and crystallised round and oval sweets. Presents for the assembled family were on small tables. These included the gifts which I had painted, embroidered or crocheted at school.

Children were expected to produce Christmas tributes for their elders and before I could explore my own presents there were things I had to do.

I had copied in my very best writing poems in French and German. These were on gaudily decorated paper which had been given to us at school. I handed the sheets of paper to my mother with a curtsy, stood back and recited; then I had to play my latest piano pieces, and then, at last, I could look at my presents.

On my table was always a Playbox Annual sent by my father and some book from Nellie and Jeannie. My mother never spoke German with us, so I had not forgotten how to speak and read English, and the annual, recalling to me my eagerly awaited Rainbow comic which had come every week at Shortwood, formed a tenuous link with the child I had once been and reminded me that somewhere, in strange surroundings impossible to visualise, my father still existed.

There was no pagan feasting and gorging connected with this peaceful festival. If I had been old enough to stay up to dinner, I would have eaten the traditional carp – a fish which I discovered much later to taste of mud and to be full of sharp bones. Christmas Day was restful and quiet and we spent it enjoying our presents undisturbed.

Then came the New Year with its own symbols: pigs, chimney sweeps and four-leafed clover – all bringers of luck. My mother had told me how in her young days real chimney sweeps in their coal-black clothes and skull caps, carrying ladders and flue brushes, had walked the streets on New Year's Eve and kissed the unwary to bring them luck, and real piglets were let loose to run about and squeal and bring luck to the town. We only saw them as toy figures with bags of sweets, or as charms enclosed in lockets.

The custom we enjoyed most was lead pouring. All Pat's broken lead soldiers or animals were collected through the year in a special tin and on New Year's Day put over a spirit stove till the paint bubbled off and burnt away in a spout of acrid black smoke and only silvery lead remained in the tin. Then, carefully with a special spoon, we poured spoonfuls of the lead into a basin of water. It hissed and contorted itself into fantastic shapes. These were omens of what would happen to us in the New Year. We didn't believe this really, but treasured the silver ships, wreathes or animals for a few weeks, after which they were put back into the tin to wait for next year's lead-pouring.

Easter came with the short Viennese spring when trees were suddenly full of clean green leaves and the parks full of violets and celandine. Easter eggs appeared in our breakfast table – not just chocolate but bright cardboard ones too, with toys inside. I remember the most splendid of them all which held a school of Easter hares with blackboard, desks and a schoolmaster in spectacles. On Easter Sunday we would go for an outing into the Prater or to the fresh woods and meadows of the Wienerwald.

There is one more festival which I must describe and for this one I was not a participant but a very serious onlooker. Whitsun was the time when children were confirmed. When they came out from the churches they processed round the town in open carriages, the girls beautifully dressed in frilly white, their hair in ringlets wreathed with white flowers or tied with white ribbons, the boys in smart, new dark suits. As I watched the cortège which, after driving through some of the main streets, headed for the Prater and roundabouts and icecreams, I recognised schoolfriends, who, overcome by the occasion were too solemn to wave. For that short, sunny afternoon I felt English, alien and excluded.

4

F OR THE LONG summer holidays, which lasted three
months, Aunt Mitzi rented a peasant farmer's
house in Altaussee in the Salzkammergut.

In those days it was a remote village, difficult to
reach, for it had no railway station and the road led over
a very steep pass.

We arrived by train in Bad Aussee, a small town some miles away where we, with our luggage, transferred into a horse-drawn carriage which carried us slowly up the hill beside the river Traun, jumping and tumbling to meet us, in its boulder-strewn bed. The pure sweet air off the mountains had already begun to intoxicate us through the windows of the train. To this was now added the smell of pine needles, woodsmoke, horse, cow and goat.

The carriage eventually pulled up in front of a three-storey wooden house with large balconies one above the other along the whole length of one side. Small fields rose in terraces behind it until they met the forest on the lower slopes of the Loser, a mountain which rose to rocky pinnacles and dominated one side of the lake.

Pat was always wildly excited when we arrived and ran about and turned somersaults on the grass. He remained out of hand for several days. I was quietly happy and fell blissfully asleep to the noise of the Traun rushing and bubbling on the other side of the road which led up towards the pass between the Loser and its neighbour the Sandling.

I awoke early to a sound which was to wake me every morning of our long summer holiday: the goat-boy coming up the road blowing his cow's horn and stopping for the goats which peasants brought out of stables and sheds and let loose into the large herd already collected. Bleating and pattering they disappeared up the stony road. On a clear day we could sometimes see them high up on the hanging meadows of the Loser and hear the tiny tinkle of their bells. Towards evening they came down again, the boy blowing his horn and the goats, of their own accord turning aside in twos and threes to find their owner or making their own way back to their stalls.

The village cows spent the summer on the high pastures round the Alm[3] huts. Women moved up into the mountains with them and were visited by their men and by mountaineers who would stop for drinks of milk fresh from the cow, or sour, cold and very refreshing.

The lake lay deep and dark in a hollow between the Loser, the Trisselwand and the Tressenstein. The Trisselwand was a sheer, rocky wall, higher than the Loser, the Tressenstein low, wooded and boring. At the village end of the lake where it flowed out into a river which joined the Traun, the land became open and rolling towards distant and far higher mountains; the furthest and highest of them all, the Dachstein, its glacier white and shining as the Celestial City, or shrouded in black and menacing clouds, seemed the symbol of another world.

Before long I found out that mountains, although most of the time like dear familiar friends, each with their name and individual character, could be fierce and sinister. Sometimes they reverberated with great thunderstorms, were full of hauntings, and indeed they could kill.

------

[3] Alpine meadow.

When walking round the lake or on some mountain track, we would come across little wooden shrines. They had crudely painted pictures protected by wooden roofs, and were nailed to trees. They showed with figures as simple as if they had been painted by children, exactly how fatal accidents had happened: a man pushed over a precipice by a cow, hit by a falling tree, or falling through the ice of the lake. Rumours of ghosts and mysterious disappearances were whispered by the peasants and passed on to us by Gecki or by my friend Mitzerl the daughter of the owner of our house.

The mountains did not always need the help of cows or trees to do their killing: a man named Alexander vanished mysteriously on the Trisselwand. Several years later his skeleton was found just below the common track where it crossed sheer walls of rock. There he had lain only a few yards from where cheerful holiday makers passed to and fro. So another ghost was added to the mountains and Gecki took us to see the grave where his sad remains were buried.

Then there was the tragedy of a servant girl who had been cruelly turned away by her mistress for misbehaviour and had tried to cross the moraine-strewn path between the Trisselwand and the Loser. Her cries had been heard all night by the peasants who had a house at the far end of the lake, but by morning, when a search party had been called, she was dead. For several nights I could not sleep for hearing her cries in my waking dreams.

Many of the peasants in Alt Aussee had large houses like the one in which we stayed which they let to summer visitors, and a great number of them were rented by members of my family or their friends. The beautiful surroundings lightened everybody's spirits and we met so often in each other's houses, in the streets or shops, at Uncle Edmund's swimming hut by the lake or in our favourite café, that the holiday seemed like one long party. Groups would gather for outings: long walks in the mountains or shorter ones to well known viewpoints and the children would often go on these too.

Uncle Edmund, splendid in leather shorts and a white shirt which matched his beard and hair, was a great leader of exhibitions. Aunt Irene, who wore peasant costume as we all did, looked more beautiful than ever in its tight bodice and full skirt, apron and silk fringed scarf. She wore handmade silver brooches, earrings and finger rings, but did not usually come on our expeditions as she was not fond of swimming or walking far.

The peasant dress was very traditional and very little like the theatrical versions which later became fashionable for foreigners at the Salzburg Festival. It was so natural for summer visitors to wear it that anything else would have made us look conspicuous and overdressed. I loved mine – bodice, wide skirt and apron would all be different but with carefully matched colours and patterns, as would the neck scarf. Under the bodice we wore white blouses with low necks and puffed sleeves. This was the Aussee Dirndl, other valleys had different ones. The light free feeling of its swinging skirt was part of the joy of being in Aussee.

Mausi and her family were also often in Aussee. We would be together a great deal and when the days of stinging hot sunshine were brought to an end, as they always were, by fierce and fearful thunderstorms and two or three days of uninterrupted rain spun out of the clouds like a forest of grey ropes, I put on my loden cape and splashed through the rain to Mausi's house where we played long games of cards, lotto and later, Mah Jong.

The friend with whom I was almost inseparable was Mitzerl, the peasant girl. She was very close to my age and had moved with her family out of the big house into a much smaller one in the garden, until in the autumn when we left for Vienna, they moved back to spend the winter in the big house. She had straw coloured, strangely matt hair, a wide simple face, and ran about barefoot on hardened feet. When it was wet or cold she wore clogs – wooden soles with leather toe caps, over thick woollen socks. The clogs could be seen at house doors in graded rows from father's to two-year-old's – only socks were worn indoors.

We played dolls and hospitals among the bushes, or spent hours making complicated villages in the dry powdery earth, for families of small sticks. Gecki would take Mitzerl with us for walks, and swimming in the lake.

Each summer we picked up instantly where we had left off the year before. From her I discovered what peasant life in Aussee was like, and there were many things I envied. Particularly I wanted to see Aussee in all the seasons: the mountains golden in autumn, the landscape disguised by snow in winter. I should have loved to have gone to school on skis and tobogganed down the slopes. I knew that ferocious avalanches crashed down the Loser in the spring – I had seen their trail of destruction in the woods – and I could imagine all the flowers in the meadow as the snow melted. When the summer visitors had left, life became very simple. The cows and goats were stalled and all provisions gathered in and stored. It was not till later that winter sports enriched the peasants and made them more sophisticated.

The Salzkammergut is a region where salt had been mined from pre-Roman times and about a mile from the village was Aussee's own salt mine. I visited it and slid down into its depths on a rather terrifyingly steep chute and walked for a whole afternoon round its glittering galleries and underground lakes. In a small museum I had seen stone lamps and iron tools which Romans and perhaps earlier people had left behind.

Many of the men in Aussee were salt miners and Mitzerl's brother Pepperl worked there when he left school. After Austria had been annexed by the Nazis and liberated by the Allies, the peasants of Aussee led the occupying officers to the salt mine and showed them paintings from the great National Gallery in Vienna which had been stored there. Their quick action prevented these treasures from being destroyed by the

Nazi rearguard. I was happy that Pepperl and other friends of my childhood had helped to save my much loved paintings from the Kunsthistorisches Museum.

It was in the lake at Aussee that I first became brave enough to take my foot off the bottom and swim. At the far end where the meadows were flat and silt caused the ground to slope very gradually, I walked out into the lake until the water felt buoyant enough, and gave myself to it. From then on swimming became a passionate occupation and no depth or temperature, not even the thousands of little fishes which darted about in thick clusters in the shallower water, could keep me from swimming wherever and whenever I was allowed.

There were also boats to be hired; rowing boats and a variety of gondola which was found locally and nowhere else except Venice, and at the end of summer there was a lake festival. A band blasted and and thumped marches and Ländler[4] by the lakeside and everyone, including ourselves, danced and twirled and slapped our thighs.

In the evening little boats were hired out and hung with paper lanterns which glowed in the gathering dusk; we hung Chinese lanterns in the trees in our gardens and the moon came up and added its light to the simple prettiness around us.

The biggest festival came when the days began to draw in and the summer landscape almost imperceptibly

---

[4] Country dance tunes.

began to take on the colours and smells of autumn. On the eve of the Kirtag which was the patronal festival of the church, wooden booths were put up on either side of the winding road which led past the only real hotel. We saw lovely things being unpacked and piled up and our excitement grew more and more so that when we were taken home and put to bed, we could only sleep fitfully. For the Kirtag was like Christmas – everyone bought and exchanged small presents.

Although grownups sometimes cheated and gave each other things which they had brought from Vienna or from the more sophisticated shops in Bad Aussee, everything else came off the stalls. In those days all the gifts were locally made, bright and simple: there were piles of gingerbread hearts, houses, dolls and animals. They were piped with coloured sugar and had paper mottoes and love messages stuck on them. There were wooden boxes of all sizes and shapes, spoons, pin cushions, frames, pen holders, all decorated with poker work and with bright Alpine flowers painted on them. There were, too, wooden hearts with sometimes rather suggestive messages. There were Tyrolean rings of Baroque patterned silver, brooches and necklaces finely carved from bone, and bracelets and all kinds of carnival toys: trumpets, streamers and balloons. Some of the stalls had more utilitarian things like wooden barrels and buckets, knives and scythes. As we sauntered up and down the road closely guarded by Gecki, with Mitzerl who, like me, had brought a doll with her, dressed in its smartest clothes, everyday life was obliterated and the carnival prevailed.

The following morning the stalls had vanished and only scraps of wood, shavings and coloured paper chased by the wind were there to remind us of what had been.

The air grew cooler day by day until the time came for us to pack, load the carriage and say goodbye to Mitzerl and her family for another year. As we drove towards Bad Aussee it was the mountains that I was beginning to grieve for, they seemed gradually to be turning their backs on me and I fought back tears. Then I remembered Sasie who had stayed behind in Vienna and my feelings quickly changed to longing for her.

AFTER FOUR YEARS of living in Vienna, when I was nearly ten, my mother had got back some of the money which she had forfeited during the war and my father was showing some signs of settling down in a job. We moved, with Sasie, to Baden bei Wien, a small town fifty miles outside Vienna. This town, which had formerly been a fashionable spa, had a certain elegance in its centre and roads with quite large houses with gardens on its outskirts.

I was soon plunged into a new school and although I missed my Hanausek friends I was much happier there. It was a girls' Lyceum and I started in the preliminary class. The building had four storeys and echoing staircases and at break we clattered down the stone stairs and into a courtyard. When we thought no-one was looking we escaped into a street and bought pink, very sweet banana shaped biscuits from a small shop.

The children were from very varied backgrounds: farms, shops and stately town houses. My special friend was Stella, a fat little girl, daughter of an American who was originally from Hungary. She spoke English with a strangely mixed accent which I soon picked up, to the horror of my father who had come to stay with us. He was in general dismayed at how un-English I had become. We told tales[5] at school quite naturally and more out of a sense of order than with any feelings of spite, for there were no punishments – only reprimands. I had also boasted to him that I ran fast enough to get away from some tough boys who threw stones at me on my walk to school. Run away? English girls don't do that! I was very puzzled. Should I have stood still and let myself be mobbed? I continued to run.

The country came very close to our home in Baden. We lived in a ground floor flat and were allowed to play in the garden, which was small but had some interesting corners where I could hide myself and act out stories. The road outside soon stopped having houses along it, became a country track and wooded hills overlooked us and there were meadows which in the spring were full of grape hyacinths.

On the low hills either side of the road stood ruined castles. I became absorbed in their legends and our young maid told me that as I was a Sunday's child, if I went up

---

[5] *i.e.* sneaked on each other.

to one of the castles very early on a Sunday morning I would see the knights and the ladies as they had been long ago. How I wished that I could steal out, but it would have been impossible to escape from my mother and Sasie.

There were other legends which absorbed my imagination and waking dreams, for it was at this time that Fritz Lang's beautiful film of the Nibelung Saga came to our cinemas. It was based on the medieval German epic and had more coherence and historical reality than Wagner's version, though magic was still very much part of it. All of my class at school became wrapped up in the moving and tragic story, acted it in our free time and collected postcards from it which were in all the stationers' shops. I had an almost superstitious reluctance to ask for anything I wanted, however badly, so I just longed and longed.

One day when, as usual, I had passed a shop and gazed at the pictures I wanted most and longed for them all the way home, I found that dear Aunt Lily Zingarelli had come out from Vienna to visit us and had brought me six of the most beautiful of the cards. After that my collection soon grew, as my mother and Sasie gave me one or the other when I had been especially good or had a good mark at school. We all took our cards to school and compared them. One day I lost some and several days later caught sight of them in the desk of a lively curly headed girl. I didn't say anything – it would have been difficult to prove and I didn't want to make trouble.

At the time I was handing my autograph album round to each of my classmates in turn and when this little girl returned it she had written in it the usual rather moralising verse which in her case urged me to enjoy life and not long for those things which were snatched from me. I'm sure she was too young to have intended the irony deliberately.

We stayed in Baden for about a year – I remember the crunch of autumn leaves in the avenues as I shuffled and stamped on my walks to and from school. Round about Christmas I was discovered by a Dutch family that lived near us and taken to a small Protestant church hidden away among tall town houses. Here I was taught Christmas hymns and dressed as a very Baroque angel with my shining gold curls tied by a silver ribbon, a long lacy dress and fat wings, made of real feathers, reaching right down to the ground.

Spring came, with excursions through the flowery meadows, and then we were on the move once more. Unquestioning, I again left all my friends, the gentle fair-haired young teacher of whom I had grown fond, and my much loved relations. Even the sadness of parting from Sasie only gradually overcame me. The interest of setting out on a long journey prevented me from realising just what was happening.

At the start of the train journey from Vienna to Ostend I took out a book which I had been given as a leaving present. It was full of stories about dogs. Rabies was endemic in Austria and I had never before thought of asking for a pet but now I wondered whether my father, who loved animals, might buy a dog for me. Thus I began in my mind to fill the unknown which lay ahead, with something of my own to love.

6

OUR JOURNEY to England was in the early summer. My father had made no arrangements to meet us or to find anywhere for us to live and it was my Aunt Ethel who had offered to take us in. She was married to Harry Beecham, brother of Thomas, the conductor. With Beecham money[6] they were living in Lympne Castle which stands above Romney Marsh, a building very largely of Victorian Gothic but with one wing of the original, haunted, medieval castle still standing and in use. So accustomed was I becoming to moving in and out of other people's backgrounds and lives that I had begun to take it for granted, but in the night, listening to the wind moaning over the marsh, I wept bitterly for Sasie.

Aunt Ethel was very fair and pretty and also gifted and she had been frustrated in an ambition towards the stage. She wrote very lively and successful plays for the local children to act and produced them herself.

---

[6] From the 'Beecham's Pills' company.

Uncle Harry was dark and romantic looking. The Beecham fortunes had been started by a grandfather who had sold pills in Manchester market. Aunt Ethel's keen imagination invented a connection with the Medici and the Medici coat of arms – Pills Rampant, she called it – and the darkly foreign good looks of Harry and Thomas made the notion less absurd than it might have been.

There were five Beecham cousins – four boys and Audrey, the eldest and the same age as I was. She was at boarding school and only came back at weekends, so the close friendship which grew between us did not start on this first visit. Michael, very close to Audrey in age, was also away at school most of the time. He insulted Pat, who wore his hair in the sort of bob which in England only the royal children had, by thinking he was a girl. My mother was given no peace until she took him to Hythe to have it cut in a more manly style. The third child, Derrick, just younger than Pat, was fair and very like me to look at. He was musical and at this time Uncle Harry's favourite. This, and the fact that he was ostracised by the older children, who couldn't be bothered with him, and too old for the 'nursery' where he was unbearably bossy, gave him an unhappy childhood. The nursery consisted of Paul and Christopher. Paul was a sweet natured little boy of whom I quickly grew fond. Pat and I were handed over to the Nanny to take for walks and here I had my first experience of an English Sunday, for we were not allowed to desecrate the Sabbath by picking wayside flowers. I also had a very different experience on these walks: one day, it may have been a Sunday, for Audrey was with us, she begged to be taken to see a rat hunt. Men and boys were gathered together in the rick yard with stout sticks in their hands, and yapping terrier dogs bounded about. The rats which scurried out of the remains of the ricks to be beaten to death, or tossed in the air for the dogs, have remained to haunt me. The others seemed unmoved but then so, outwardly, did I.

My father remained away from us and as we could not stay too long with the Beechams, we moved into a boarding house in Herne Bay, which even today has not changed very much and was then the epitome of a small seaside holiday town with a front of early Victorian hotels and boarding houses staring out onto the cold waves of the North Sea. For the first time, I swam in the sea. Water, even though cold, was my element and I found the crashing waves and rough salt taste exhilarating in its contrast to the free and dreamy stillness of the lakes of Styria.

I also discovered Woolworths, where everything could be had for either 3d or 6d. We bought spades and buckets and cashboxes for our change. The English weather, so moody and unreliable, fascinated me. I would see a small patch of blue sky from my bed when I woke, but by breakfast time it could be raining.

My father must have sent some sort of signal to us, for we left Herne Bay after a few weeks and met him in London. Even then he had done nothing about a house and we spent several very uncomfortable nights in a room in a bed-and-breakfast house. There were two single beds which had to be pushed together and I lay over the crack between them. This and the constant arguing of my parents prevented me from sleeping.

Eventually we found a furnished house in a small road parallel to the south bank of the Thames at East Molesey. It had a very small garden – just a patchy lawn surrounded by unweeded flower beds. My imagination could scarcely transform it, but in the house itself I found treasure. Amongst the books in the poky little sitting room the owners had left a complete set of Children's Encyclopedias. They were full of interesting and lovely things. The stories of E. Nesbit which were serialised there bore me away into a world of fantasy which was a great refuge and consolation. For the quarrels between my parents often lasted all night and I lay wakeful and worried for many hours.

My wish for a dog came true: my father owned a little old-fashioned Sealyham called Peggy. She had a white woolly face, black nose and bright button eyes. At first she pined for him since he was away all day, and was only happy lying on his cap on his armchair. Soon she made friends with us and I could play with her and love her.

We had a young Irish maid called Josie and, remembering Nellie, I treated her as one of the family and hugged and kissed her until one day my mother forbade it.

If I was to be ready to go to school, it was necessary for me to learn such things as English history and weights and measures. My mother found a governess called Miss Bell to come to us daily. Pat too had to be started on writing, reading and sums. Miss Bell was an elderly retired woman who dressed rather elaborately and unfashionably in black. She had, as she reminded us constantly, been with the Chamberlains.[7] She had her own methods and we learnt the kings and queens of England to the rhythm of physical exercises. She also, surprisingly, taught us to rinse our hands in the flushing water after we had used the lavatory. This astounded my mother as we could only assume she had taught it to the Chamberlains too. Although we were shown how to do it with great care, it still seemed a strange habit to have been found in one of the foremost homes in England.

Miss Bell took us for walks to Hampton Court every day and I soon knew about Henry VIII, Wolseley and Catherine Howard and it seemed only the day before yesterday that they had left the palace, where echoes of their tragedies remained in the haunted corridors. The gloom of the Tudor building brightened into Wren's wing and I learnt the different architecture with my eyes and my imagination long before I knew the terminology. The gardens which varied so much, from the knot gardens and beautiful herbacious borders, to the Home

---

[7] The family of the politicians Joseph and Neville Chamberlain.

Park with ducks on the water and deer in the rides, were full of just invisible presences and I was grateful to Miss Bell for taking us there and letting me absorb and enjoy it in my own way.

At the end of the school holidays I was sent to a small school in East Molesey for the summer term. Although we did pay a small fee, it was very like a Board School, with small neo-Gothic buildings, heavy dark wood linings to the rooms and rows of worn and old-fashioned desks. Boys and girls were divided from each other by a partition and played in separate halves of the concrete playground. The lessons would have been dreary if schoolwork in English hadn't been so new to me. The children accepted me with my slightly strange accent – probably because none of them spoke standard English themselves.

Our little street was a small loop which began and ended in the Thames-side road. As there was no through traffic we were allowed to play in it. I had saved all my birthday and Christmas gold sovereigns, and decided to spend them on a bicycle. I had been given bicycle rides by the father of friends in Baden and just reached the stage of wobbling along by myself, so my father promised to order me one in London. So days and weeks of the summer term I spent eagerly waiting, and watching every bicycle rider who passed me. I longed for the sensation of bowling along on two wheels. My father was procrastinating and unreliable as ever, but this looking forward seemed to heighten my pleasure.

Eventually the bicycle did arrive and I spent many happy summer hours learning to ride it properly.

I got to know other children in the road and the most important to me was a little girl who lived opposite us. She had cerebral palsy, could not talk and was wheeled out in a large wheelchair. I was drawn to her by her fragility and her mother asked me to go for walks with them. In those days it was not understood that children with cerebral palsy were as intelligent as other people. Jean could only grin, gesticulate and make incomprehensible sounds, but this did not seem to be a barrier and I was happy in her company and felt that she enjoyed me being with her.

Her father had made her a large doll's house and every day he brought her back some little things from London, where he went to work. It was on a table and with Jean in her special chair and myself next to her, I played to her and felt in complete harmony.

It was a delight to have the Thames just round the corner from where we lived. Pat and I bought ourselves cheap fishing rods and fished for tiddlers and watched the pleasure steamers passing. There was also a place in the shallows where I went to swim. The ground was muddy and smelt of rotting weeds but it was yet another experience of my own element.

Before the summer was over, we had moved into a house in Ormond Avenue, Hampton and in September I started at my new school, Summerleigh in Teddington.

Lincoln House was a stuccoed and partly timbered suburban house in an avenue of similar ones. It was larger than the house in Molesey and in a 'better' neighbourhood. A spare plot next door had been added to the garden, which made it twice as large as those of our neighbours. The field on the opposite side of the road had at that time not been built on, and this gave us an almost country outlook. We owned the house and furnished it partly with new 'period' furniture but also with some from my mother's childhood rooms in Vienna. We were reunited with the things left from the sale of Shortwood. My old dolls were there, displaced in my affections by the ones who had shared my life in Austria.

The little school in Molesey had not had a uniform but now I was taken to Bentalls to be fitted out for Summerleigh, with all that was typical of an English schoolgirl, but new and exciting to me. From my 'Chilprufe' underwear to my navy mac, my shining wellingtons and satchel, everything pleased me.

In spite of the uniform, Summerleigh was far from being a conventional school and although we wore our tunics and white blouses for gym and games, for everyday we wore our ordinary clothes covered by a butcher-blue overall.

The headmistress was a Swiss woman called Madame Mottu. Her face was yellow and wrinkled as a dried fig and she had lively dark eyes and a pouting rather pendulous mouth. Black hair was piled on top of her head and her small body was draped in layers of loose dark skirts, jumpers and cardigans. Her age was a topic of rumour and legend – said to have celebrated her seventieth birthday some time before my arrival, she celebrated it again during my time at the school, though whether now she really was seventy, or even older, we could not tell. It must be remembered that in my youth seventy-five was thought really old. Madame's hair was completely and naturally black as I discovered when I was ill and put to bed in a room off her bedroom.

When I first went to Summerleigh, Monsieur Mottu was still alive. He was one of those grey old gentlemen with a drooping moustache, of the kind which in those days seemed to be everywhere. He could be seen walking slowly round the garden followed by an ancient Dandy Dinmont called Bony. Soon after, they both died and Bony had a grave in the garden, marked by a stone.

The Mottus had three daughters all married to Englishmen. Miss Marguerite, as she was still called at school, taught us the piano. She was middle-aged and chic with a pleasing French accent. I learnt with her and would have liked to have played well but the co-ordination of my hands did not come easily to me. I practised conscientiously, passed a few exams and, once I knew a piece, could play it pleasingly. By that time everybody was tired of it.

Miss Camille was married to a Cambridge professor and came once a week to teach Elocution. She also produced our plays. These were near-professional and took place in the Town Hall on several nights, with tickets sold for charity. My first year she put on A.A. Milne's *Make Believe*. This needed a large family of children and for some reason, although I did not learn Elocution, she chose me to act one of the boys.

In an Eton suit, my hair stuck down with oil, I appeared in the first act on a rocking horse. It was not until I spoke my one line that my parents recognised me. I had one more line in the last act and there must have been something spirited in the way I said them, for Miss Camille invited me to come to her classes free of charge. I loved the reciting and acting that followed and was useful in French plays, which true to the tradition of the school she brought before them at intervals.

French was very important at Summerleigh. Madame soon singled me out and in spite of my newness made me a French prefect. I had to sit at the 'French table' at lunch and talk, but it brought me no privileges.

I found the school work easy – sometimes boringly so. French lessons were particularly dull. Any book we were reading I finished in one or two lessons, turning the pages surreptitiously, then had to wait a term or more till the rest of the form caught up. I was also quite good at games and sports – probably because I was tall for my age.

When I arrived at the school, one of three new girls in my form, the rest of the form were in the process of making a gang under the leadership of a girl called Beryl. Of course we were excluded and hung about, an ill assorted bunch. Fortunately the gang soon broke up and by that time I was already making friends and starting my own imaginative game, which drew in many of the former gang. For a short time I was teased about my accent. When I told the girls that I had been living in Austria I discovered that they had never heard of it and thought I meant Australia.

It was during my first term that we were asked to write something for the school magazine. I had never heard of such a thing and imagined it like the magazines I bought at the newsagents in Hampton – glossy and illustrated. I was very eager to have something in print and wrote my first poem. It was published and I won the Junior Poetry Prize – a copy of Scott's *The Talisman*. I did not mind that the magazine was small, thinner than an exercise book and not a bit glossy.

Beryl too wrote and she won the Junior Prose Prize. It was she who soon after that discovered that books could be bought in junk shops for a few pence. From then on most of my pocket money was spent on books. I began to read everything in our not very large collection at home and discovered the joys of a library, for in the corner of one of the very plain class rooms was the Junior Library. Every week we were allowed to change our book and library day acquired for me a special flavour of anticipation. I read frenetically and sometimes finished a book on the day that I had taken it out. Here I found more E. Nesbit, Rider Haggard, John Buchan, Stanley Weyman and many others. I particularly loved books with a historical setting.

Meanwhile life at home was becoming very disturbing. My father began to spend more and more time at the pub. We never knew when he would come home, he missed meals or was late; there were always quarrels which went on deep into the night. I did not at that time realise that the young women he sometimes brought home were mostly a good deal more than just friends.

My mother started confiding in me. This put me in a state of perpetual underlying strain, for I was fond of my father who used to joke with me and enjoy my company. My English nature responded to his, and I could sense his irritation with my mother who had little sense of humour and was quite incapable of appreciating the good in him. I was only eleven when all this started and had to try to push it to the back of my mind and enjoy everything good that came my way.

The large amount of reading that I did gave me one of my great escapes – the escape into my imagination. Beryl's gang, I had discovered, was a game of a secret kingdom. This so fascinated me that I started one of my own: I became King of Marshland and took my father's name James. From then on Marshland was almost as real to me as my daily life. It was a place of justice, mercy and courage, with the poetry, chivalry and colour of the Middle Ages. It had a real place too – a very small island in the Thames, but a vast imaginary place also. The people in it were both real and unreal, for its princes, dukes and duchesses, its huntsmen and pages were all my favourite people in real life – Pat and his friends and girls of all ages at school. The Queen was one of the mistresses.

These all gave a reality to the game, for I told the people of their roles which were so like their characters, that they never refused me. I suppose most children live a great deal in their imagination and I had discovered a way which overflowed at times and in differing degrees into theirs. It made me many friends and no enemies, for although there were some whom I cast as villains they were not told. Beryl did not relinquish her place as king of her own kingdom but we became allies and friends.

My mother was developing a state of mind which saw all men as unimaginative brutes who only liked women if they were pretty and had no brains. Dangerous as this could have been for me, it had two great advantages: she encouraged me to be independent, and to join the Girl Guides. I took myself to and from school at first by tram and later on my bicycle and on foot with my special friends. We explored the Royal Parks of Hampton Court, Bushey and Richmond, the banks of the Thames and spots of wilderness which still existed amongst the houses and factories.

My mother had brought with her from Vienna a Girl Guide Handbook, which must have been one of the first to be published. I was fascinated by the accounts of fire making, signalling, camping, the enjoyment of nature and the many ways in which girls could be independent of, or of service to others. I eagerly joined the school company, was given my uniform as a Christmas present and longed for accidents or emergencies that might let me show how well I was prepared.

One of my closest friends was Nancy Charles, daughter of the vicar of Hampton. Her father was elderly and rather silent and dry, her mother much younger, a beautiful dark-haired woman who suffered much from her nerves and spent most of the day lying on her bed or on a couch downstairs. Nancy was older than me, tall and long legged with large blue eyes and a gold 'rat-trap' in her mouth, and in a higher form at school. We did not have much to do with each other there but in the holidays we were inseparable.

We spent a lot of the time in her large vicarage nursery with its very plain furniture and barred windows, or, when her father was out, sitting on the floor in front of a coal fire in his dark, heavily furnished study. She was my chief Marshland friend and I carried her off into my imagination. But there were many other things we enjoyed together. We cleaned out and fed our families of guinea pigs, observed birds and flowers and kept nature diaries, giggled and never grew tired of each other's company.

Another friend, half Italian, was always known as Bobby, for she was stocky and boyish. Her mother was English, kind and cosy; they lived in a large house with a rambling garden. She was the youngest of a family of four and had a sister and two brothers – Josefina, Vittorio and Eduardo. These romantic sounding names became for every day Josie, Victor and Ted. The large unkempt garden sloped down to a brook which we explored in an old dinghy. There were waterfowl and water rats, and it is still part of the furniture of my imagination and comes to my mind's eye when I think of Tennyson's poem 'I come from haunts of coot and hern...'. It is also my setting for *The Wind in the Willows*, among many other poems and books that I was reading at that time. Bobby and I played dance records and gossiped about people at school.

There were other friends who asked me to tea and I loved going into their houses which mostly seemed very peaceful, conventional and safe compared to mine. I needed the respite, but I don't think that I would have chosen to have their more boring backgrounds if I had been given the chance, for I was beginning to appreciate what a truly English character my father was, with his love of horses and dogs and the English countryside. Even his drinking and womanising, and certainly his sense of humour were English in a way which would have been more fitting in a novel by Sterne or Defoe than in the 'modern' twenties.

I now came to a far more complicated time of my life, when Marshland, which had been the expression in my imagination of my loves and friendships started to be of less importance. The tangles of adolescence began where love was complex and the pursuit of justice blurred.

My father spent most of his day away from home. He had some kind of work in London, but most evenings was in the Red Lion at Hampton or in the Mitre at Hampton Court. He often went to the races and even at weekends, when we had made plans to drive into the country or to the sea for picnics, he kept us waiting and sometimes stayed away altogether. My mother began to take on a martyred look and I was torn between them both, for my temperament drew me towards the more life-affirming character of my father and I resented the degree to which my mother despised him.

Once we had stayed in England, Sasie came to stay with us for many months every year. I loved her as much as ever and missed her sadly when she went home to Switzerland, but she too criticised my father and showed no understanding when I spoke up for him. The tension made me rude and pert. It came to a climax when for the first time I felt myself to be on my own and forced into a position where I knew that however I tried I would no longer be able to be loving and kind to these three people in the same way as I had been before. So much was I being torn from every side that I knew I would have to use all the strength I had within me to create some sort of defensive barrier. With real sadness I retreated into a reserve which I had never before felt necessary.

So my life at Hampton was led against an almost unbroken background of stress. Night after night I would be woken by angry voices from my parents' bedroom. For hours I lay awake with my heart thudding. Once or twice, when my mother came near the end of her endurance she disappeared and we had no notion where she was. I lived these days in fear and oppression which even my enjoyment of school could not lift. After a few days in London, during which she sent no message, she would return.

Pat, fortunately, was a weekly boarder at his prep. school and missed a great deal of the strain. I loved him and tried to keep things cheerful for him, but the difference between our ages was beginning to tell. I spent most of my time at home reading – he was getting too old for the sort of games I had invented for him.

There were other signs that I was growing up. For some time Bobby had been teasing me about the interest I had shown in her brothers. At first it was Victor who, with his dark Italian looks, became a romantic figure for me. He was nearly twenty-one and too old for me to expect any response other than kindly interest, though I was invited to his coming-of-age dance to keep Bobby company. It was the first grownup dance I had been to and it was more or less as a spectator that I moved amongst the young people in their dinner jackets and dresses with skirts well above the knees and belts low down on their hips. The tunes were mostly catchy and cheerful foxtrots and Charlestons and kind Victor danced with me several times.

Soon after that I began to feel a real tenderness for Ted – not nearly so good looking but a serious sixteen year old with horn rimmed spectacles. We used to go into his room where he sat painting. To my joy, he came up to me in the garden one afternoon, and gave me a red carnation. Its deep colour and velvet smell seemed the very epitome of love.

After that Bobby became the bearer of letters between us. Sadly for me, Ted's love for me was not as purely romantic as mine for him. He was not content with letters but wanted me to steal out and meet him. I could not face acting and lying to my parents and Sasie, so I had to write and tell him it was not possible. For some time our letters went on but then the little affair died for lack of encouragement, though Ted, for long after, was the man in my imagination.

Another young man who influenced me in those days was Willy, who came over from Vienna to visit us. My mother had often taken us round picture galleries but it was Willy who first awoke the pleasure I was to find in paintings. I was sent with him to the National Gallery and he explained the differences in the schools of painting. He spent a long time introducing me to famous artists and pictures and I came away entranced: looking at pictures with a good looking and lively young man was such fun that I became instantly converted to everything he showed me.

During this time, when I was entering my teens, my father, having failed at his job in London, persuaded my mother to invest some of her money in a riding school near Hampton Court. In stables that had once belonged to the Mitre Hotel, he installed some suitable ponies and horses, which included hunters for himself and his friends.

Naturally he encouraged Pat and myself to ride. I found that I had completely forgotten all that I had learnt at Shortwood and with a milder and gentler groom to teach me I soon reached enough skill and confidence to take my favourite pony into the Parks. In my smart Harry Hall breeches, tweed coat and floppy hat, I would bicycle to the stables before or after school and have exhilarating gallops down the rides at Hampton Court Home Park or Bushey Park, hooves thundering on the flat turf between lines of ancient oaks.

Through the riding school even more lively young women came into my father's life. He taught them and rode out with them and took them to the races. My mother would have nothing to do with the life of the school, so he was left to their unlimited company during his working hours and in the bar of the Mitre afterwards. When I came across them they would be sweet to me and I responded to their cheerfulness and friendliness.

One girl in particular, small, pretty, with dark short curls, came more intimately into our lives. She was orphaned and rich and the model of all that was smart and 'fast' in the twenties. She wore very short skirts, painted her lips and nails a bright vermilion, smoked cigarettes through a long holder and drove a fast little sports car. Her name was Frankie and she had been jilted by one of my father's younger friends. She was the only one of his girls that my father brought home regularly. Her little girl ways made my mother accept her and I myself began to love her – she was so light hearted, warm, generous and affectionate. Often she and my father would take me out with them to the races and to fairs where Frankie enjoyed the noise and lights and swooping rides on swings and roundabouts as much as I did. She came with us on Sunday family outings and brightened them with her playfulness and chatter.

In the meantime there were two summer holidays when we went abroad and my father did not come with us. For the first of these, when I was twelve, we went back to Aussee. Months beforehand I was happily excited and hardly dared let my mind dwell on it in case something happened to stop us from going.

When we got there after an exhausting journey with many changes of train and a night in a hotel which brought me my first and only experience of bed bugs, I found that it had lost none of its enchantment. For the space of a few weeks, England and all its sadness fell away.

Many of my Austrian family were there for that summer and these included two charming boys of about my age: my distant cousins, Georg and Erich Steger. They were both very lively and good looking, with black curly hair and sparkling dark eyes, and they became my faithful followers.

Every day they called for me and we amused ourselves in a great many ways. We climbed trees and Georg was inspired to such boldness that he went farther than ever before and fell to the ground with a great thud. He lay on his back, pale and gasping, but before I could go for help he got up. He had only been badly winded. He was also fond of operating on an old teddy bear which had become limp with the matting up of his stuffing. I acted as nurse as he cut open the bear's stomach, inserted some rags and stitched him up again.

When Georg discovered that I still played with dolls and had invented a large family, whose father, my husband, I had placed in Arizona – for riding and cowboy films had affected my fantasy world – he began to argue fiercely that I should somehow eliminate this imaginary husband and have him instead. I believe I refused him because I wanted him to stay firmly in the real world and not in the world of my fantasy.

Georg and Erich both gave me wooden hearts at the Jahrmarkt,[8] with their names burnt on in pokerwork. Erich's said simply 'Your Erich', but Georg's had a saucy rhyme on it about sin on the Alm. I don't know whether

---

[8] Annual fair.

he understood its meaning – I certainly did not until much later. When we left for the station at Bad Aussee in an open carriage, both brothers ran after it and tossed me great bunches of flowers. They ran until they were too out of breath to follow us further.

Georg wrote to me in England regularly and I answered him. One day my mother said, 'Georg is in love with you.' Like the apple from the tree of knowledge, this made me self-conscious and my letters became difficult to write. The correspondence dwindled and came to an end. The second time we went abroad was to stay with Sasie where she lived on the outskirts of Lausanne. The house belonged to a market gardener whose land reached down to the edge of the lake.

I was in a dreamlike state, near to delirium at being at last in Switzerland, the fabulous land that Sasie had told me so much about in my early childhood. The great blue sparkling lake, snowy mountains, and Sasie's relations whose photos and names I had loved for so long, were real now and I could hardly get used to the idea. On one of the first days of the holiday we went for a long walk in the foothills and returned over upland meadows where we walked for several hours towards the setting sun.

During the night I began to suffer from sunstroke, became truly delirious and lived through several days when I could not tell dream from reality or nightmare. Sasie nursed me back to normal with drinks of wine and water and we had weeks of happy walks, visits and trips on the white lake steamers. Best of all we swam. I became

friends with a girl of my own age called Barbara
Whitman, who was the daughter of an American
diplomat in Geneva. She was pretty and sweet natured
and we spent whole days swimming, often underwater,
and in the sunshine tried to catch small lizards that
slipped in and out of holes in the rocks.

In the evenings, when lake and sky were black, Sasie
and I, our arms round each other, watched the steamer
cross over from the French shore. It glittered like rows of
diamonds and the stars twinkled above. At those times,
so close to Sasie, I felt happy and safe.

Going back to England always brought a feeling of
dread, though I looked forward to seeing my school
friends again.

It soon became clear that the riding school was going
to be yet another of my father's failures, for although it
was very popular it was losing money. My mother was in
a perpetual state of anxiety and I, quite unable to comfort
her, was frightened of the loss of all our money and the
desolation that she told me would probably overcome us.
My father was drinking even more than before and my
mother, giving up hope that he would ever lead the
conventional money earning life of the families around
us, decided to buy some land in the country, build a
house and let him live the life of a country gentleman.

We spent weekends driving round the Home
Counties looking at property and eventually bought a
nine acre field in Cranleigh in Surrey. It was at the foot of
the Surrey Hills, with an unspoilt view of the more

distant Hascombe Hill. An architect drew plans for a long, low white farmhouse style building, with a steeply pitched roof, stables and a large garage. While it was being built my parents planned to move into a furnished flat in Guildford.

I was very upset at the thought of leaving Summerleigh and begged to be allowed to stay on as a boarder. As Pat was to stay at his prep. school near Hampton, it was agreed that I too should not change schools.

Summerleigh consisted of two houses whose gardens had been joined. The main house was tall dark and ivy covered, and it was here that the boarders had their dormitories. There were never many and we slept in plain bare rooms with five or six to a room.

It was usual for girls from the school to leave at about fourteen and go away to boarding schools, so the number of girls whom I knew well had already grown smaller. Madame, I discovered, was relentless in her possessiveness. I was one of her favourites because I knew French and worked well, but far from my gaining any advantage, she was quite oppressive in the attention she gave to everything that I did. Afraid that we might complain, she read our letters and listened to our telephone calls. Another unexpected suffering that I discovered was that we were always short of food, and hungry. The food was indeed remarkably good, but served in portions quite insufficient for growing children.

My first term I endured fairly well – I still enjoyed the novelty and the end of term was enlivened by one of the best plays that Mrs Prior had produced, in which I had an important part. In A.P. Herbert's *Fat King Melon and Princess Caraway*, I was Mr Bloodorange the Highwayman and with my black mask, cloak and three cornered hat, I fought a triangular duel with the king and the princess, in which we each used a different sort of weapon. When the play was over, I had to say goodbye to several of my friends who were leaving, and to the mistress to whom I had been devoted for all the years I had been at school.

We passed Christmas in Guildford in the furnished flat we had rented and it was so cold that we could only spend short spells in the drawing room where the Christmas tree had been put up. Most of the time we huddled in the tiny dining room and the maid was so cold in the kitchen that she kept the gas oven lit to warm her feet. Of my presents I remember the two Pooh books and an expensive purple leather writing case, which was from Frankie. I was delighted with this and locked away in it all my most private letters and photographs.

When I returned to Summerleigh, there was only one girl with me in the senior dormitory. Zoë had been new the term before and was very different from most of the other girls, for she lived in Brighton and was very townish. She was older than me, wore high heels, more powder and lipstick than anyone else would have dared, plucked her eyebrows, and had her very dark hair beautifully cut in a sleek bob. She was bad at lessons probably because her heart was never remotely in them. She took bad marks and rebukes with careless good nature.

At home in Brighton she belonged to a group of young people who met in cafés and went to dances in hotels and had a kind of teenage worldliness, though teenagers had not yet been invented. She seemed to me sophisticated and grown up and I enjoyed the friendly confidences she shared with me and the new world she opened up. Her various experiences of love never went beyond romance and kisses, and sometimes heartbreak. It was a vivid, brightly lit world of boys and girls set against the white houses and blue sea of Brighton, which fitted well with the more modern novels of Jeffrey Farnol, in whose works I so happily lost myself at that time.

In order to bring some pleasure into the dreariness of that term, Zoë and I got permission to keep a bird. We clubbed our money together and bought some sort of a finch which we kept in a large cage on a deserted verandah. Shopping for it and feeding it gave us enjoyment, though it was not very responsive.

Some of the teachers in the upper school were very elderly and English and History, my favourite subjects, were boringly taught. Maths never inspired me, and in French and German I was still too far in advance of the class to be interested. So my former keenness for work faded. Even Guides lost its edge as I was passed over, unfairly I thought, as Second in my patrol, and my pleasure which would have been stimulated by responsibility was rather lost in resentment.

One evening when we were getting ready for bed, Zoë showed me a pocket book which her uncle, who had fought on the Somme, had found on a dead soldier. I held it and looked at it carefully: it was a small, pathetic, damaged khaki object. All that night I dreamt haunted dreams of muddy trenches, corpses and of one man who was trying to talk to me. At intervals I woke up, my teeth chattering as I shivered with cold. In the morning I couldn't get up – I had a high fever.

Madame moved me into a small room next to her bedroom, a doctor was called, I was given medicine and during the night, her long black hair streaming over her shoulders in strange contrast to her withered face, she came to watch me and bring me drinks. For many days I was too weak to take much notice of what was happening around me, as I dozed day and night.

One afternoon when I was sleeping after lunch, I woke with a start – I had heard my father's voice in the hall saying: 'Give her my love, please.' He had called to see me and bring me some books and Madame was on the point of sending him away. Desperately I sat up and shouted to him and she had to let him come to me, but from this moment onward I became frightened of her possessiveness and power. I felt helpless and imprisoned and when my father came again and I was up, I begged him to take me home and threatened to run away if he refused. He was too embarrassed at the thought of facing

Madame to do anything to help me, and I knew there was no hope of leaving before the end of term. I resigned myself and kissed him goodbye.

Madame kept up her strange malignant attitude when she received a letter from my mother after the end of term, saying that I would not be going back. She denied that I had ever been under provisional notice and even had her solicitor send several letters claiming a term's fees.

So my time at Summerleigh came to a sad end. We never heard from Madame again but I did keep my friendships with Nancy and Bobby and several other girls, and I got an occasional card from Zoë who left and returned happily to her Brighton world – she was no letter writer. Marshland had vanished, to reappear in bright fragments and at long intervals in poems. I had left another life behind me.

7

GUILDFORD in 1929 was a charming market town. Before the influx of people at the beginning of the Second World War it had a small population and there were still carts among the cars, rattling and bumping down the steep cobbled High Street. Shops, not yet disfigured by large panes of plate glass, aluminium fittings and ugly signs, were very much the same as on postcards of a hundred years earlier. I drank in the feeling of old England. It all seemed straight from a Christmas card and I could almost hear the wheels of a stage coach about to appear and clatter up the High Street from the Portsmouth Road.

Lovely country walks led from the edge of the town. The track to Loseley House which started a mile or so up the road from where we lived was one of our favourites. Sandy Lane passed through a lonely valley with an occasional farm in the wooded bottom and fields sloping up the chalk of the Hog's Back. At one point the woods parted and there stood Loseley – Elizabethan and remote. One of my father's friends told tales of a haunted room where a dog which had been left overnight was found dead, his face a mask of fear. Tenants who were not members of the family which had owned it through the centuries left after a week, so disturbing had been the ghostly noises and torments; servants hurried home before dark for fear of shadowy figures.

During the freezing Christmas holidays we tobogganed down the steep slopes of St Catherine's Hill on white rime. The chapel, ruined and romantic as an etching in a Walter Scott novel, rose above us and if we scrambled down the steep drop to the river Wey, there was a ferry which from the days of King John had carried travellers across to the continuation of the Pilgrims Way, for St Catherine's was one of the pilgrims' chapels. The cost of the ferry cannot have changed much since King John's time – it was one penny. His castle guarded the narrow cleft in the chalk at the entrance to the town. It was largely in ruins and revived in me feelings of Marshland which by this time were crystallising into what I felt for real history.

Peggy the Sealyham had died in giving birth to puppies by a mate of her own choosing who had been, sadly, of a breed too large for her. We now had a sentimental black labrador called Gyp, acquired by my father from one of his friends. I adored this dog and he came everywhere with us. He even pulled our sledge to and fro on our way to the hill. An indignant old lady scolded us for being so cruel and as we looked at Gyp's wildly wagging tail we smothered our giggles.

At the start of the Easter holidays we left Gyp with my father and Sasie and left for Vienna. We stayed with Uncle Edmund and Aunt Irene in the flat which had been my grandmother's. The weeks there were full of treats, but because our dentist at home had badly neglected my teeth, I had appointments with an Austrian one almost every morning. This man, who looked like Rasputin, was large, with a silky black beard, red lips and big soft well manicured hands. As a baby, because of some fault in my nutrition, I had suffered from rickets and my teeth were unusually sensitive, with nerves exposed in unexpected places. This man did not shout and bully me as a Viennese dentist earlier in my childhood had done, but the sessions were peculiarly painful and I endured them as a kind of ordeal to qualify me for the pleasure to come later in the day.

In the afternoon we went visiting. Lily Fluss was back from Italy, her marriage to Italo Zingarelli already broken and her beloved elder daughter Laetitia dead. Carla, the second child was four years old, dark and lively. I enjoyed this little cousin who attached herself to me and chattered away happily. 'Evelyn, I can write, shall I show you?' She scribbled indecipherably on a sheet of paper. What have you written?' I asked. 'How do I know, I can't read yet!'

I went to tea with Mausi. We had written regularly and now sat solemnly in her parents' drawing room, sipping lemon tea and eating biscuits from a tray the maid had brought in for us, as we talked about our school friends.

Georg Steger, taller and more handsome than ever, appeared and invited me to his parents' house. He was a cinema fanatic and we spent the time poring over his piles of film magazines. I knew few of his favourite film stars but was a good listener. As one film which he wanted to see was running in a fleapit cinema in the outer town, he arranged to call for me a few days later to take me to it. I can remember nothing of the film, but the fleas were very much present. I came home full of little red bites and had to have an immediate bath and change of clothes before I could be sure that I had parted company with them.

Max Perutz also asked me to his home. It was difficult to see the delicate little boy in the new, sturdy fifteen year old, already a keen mountaineer and skier. Our friendship seems uninterrupted and we were happy and easy in each other's company.

During this stay his parents gave a ball for their two older children and I was invited, to keep Max company. I wore one of the dresses my mother had made for me – black velvet with a soft white collar – and although I was not at that time really interested in clothes I felt happy amongst all the very elegantly dressed young people.

Everything was lavish and splendid: the food rich and imaginatively Viennese, and there were wonderful concoctions with birds and flowers made of ice cream. Max and I enjoyed ourselves in a half grown up, half childish way. We danced, ran around greeting the dancers and joking with them, or sat in a corner nibbling and making remarks. Many of the young people remembered me from my childhood and asked me to dance. The highlight was a cotillion.

The young men were called into another room and given posies of flowers and the girls pink muslin bags with drawstrings and our names embroidered on them.

In them were ribbon favours to pin on the young men. The band played and the men paraded in and gave their posies to their chosen girls. Of course I got Max's and pinned my favour on his lapel, but I was also given others, and soon danced off with my bag full of flowers. There was a happy family feeling at this ball as all the guests knew each other at school, through their families, or from skiing or mountaineering together. Everyone was lively but not rowdy notwithstanding the good Austrian wine.

During this holiday I had my first experience of opera. Many friends and relations had permanent bookings and it was easy to find an evening when there were seats to spare. I was taken to *Il Trovatore*, *Madame Butterfly* and *Fidelio*. At first I found operatic conventions hard to accept and rather ludicrous. I was carried along by the plot of *Il Trovatore* and enjoyed the music, but as the arias were long I had time to wonder at the absurdity of someone engaged in a secret love affair announcing his intentions in tones that ran and reverberated through the supposedly sleeping town.

The absurdities of *Madame Butterfly* quite destroyed any attempt at taking it seriously. Madame Butterfly herself was, though fittingly Japanese, a huge lady – and she sang in Italian where the rest of the cast used German. The much bewailed Pinkerton, when he finally appeared, could not have been named more aptly – he bounced in in his naval uniform, small, round and pink as a piglet. *Fidelio* overwhelmed me with the beauty of its music and story and remained for me one of the most profoundly moving of operas.

The Vienna toy shops kept their glamour for us and we discovered an excellent shop devoted entirely to jokes. There we bought dribbling glasses, swimming sugar lumps, pencils that jumped apart or made your hands filthy, and also a realistic ink blot with its bottle. This we arranged on one of Aunt Irene's dainty doilies and waited. When my mother saw it she scolded us for some five to ten minutes, until I quietly picked up the blot and put it in my pocket. Pat and I were convulsed with laughter but my mother did not think it funny at all.

When the time came for us to leave this beloved Vienna world, my mother was in a mood of deep pessimism. Not merely was she sad at leaving everybody behind, she convinced herself that many of her relations would be dead before she saw them again. As at that time none of them were really old, and there was no danger threatening them, this was absurd. We called her 'pessimistic pussy' and tried to cheer her up.

During our holiday Gyp appeared to me in a dream: I was standing by the banks of a wide river and saw him disappearing slowly on the far bank. I called him again and again and woke up sobbing. This was about half way through our stay in Vienna. When we came home we found that he had run away at this very time and we never found him again.

8

THERE WERE two girls' schools within reach of Cranleigh: one a school for young ladies in a large private house, the other, St Catherine's, the sister school of Cranleigh boys' school. I decided that I would rather go to St Catherine's, and travelled there by bus as our house in Cranleigh was not yet finished. Built as a school, it was a large H-shaped building with a small chapel at one end. Virginia creeper covered large areas of its red brick. I enjoyed the idea of such a typical school, a change from the eccentricity of Summerleigh. The large dormitories with curtained off cubicles, a vast dining room, gabled speech hall, gym, and square, plain classrooms could have come straight out of the school stories I enjoyed when I was rather younger.

We wore navy gym tunics every day and blazers with a Catherine wheel in our house colours on the breast pocket, and we had ties.

I did not settle down as quickly as I had hoped – there were few day girls and the boarders kept aloof from them. Games were all important, and of a much higher standard than at Summerleigh, but I think it was my preoccupation with the troubles at home which robbed me of all my interest and élan. In the grounds was a Giant's Stride – a post like a maypole with six ropes hanging from it. By running hard and jumping you could swing round high in the air. There was a very elaborate system of bagging ropes and manoeuvring for turns. Some daring girls even took themselves to the lavatory just before the end of lessons so that they could run out and seize a rope the moment the bell rang.

Miss Symes the headmistress was a large stately woman with grey hair parted in the middle, drawn back either side of her broad owl-like face and gathered in a bun. She had an expression of benevolent wisdom with calm, very penetrating eyes. I never grew really fond of her but respected her for her complete sense of justice. She might speak very severely if one were caught breaking a rule, but as soon as the interview was over it was all forgotten. In a school full of females where emotions often slipped over the edge of control, Miss Symes remained humorous and serene.

Our English lessons were taken by pretty, dark, lively Miss Bott. I wrote with great fluency and pleasure and Miss Bott gave me high marks and often read my essays aloud and praised me. She captivated my imagination and I became what my schoolmates called 'gone' on her. Even at the time I felt the relationship as deeper and more important than anyone else would admit. It held as much magic and torment as falling in love with men did later and sustained me through the strain of my home life. Eventually it led to a friendship full of kindness and understanding which lapsed only because Leila Bott was an incorrigibly bad correspondent.

In the summer holidays we moved into our new home in Cranleigh. I explored the fields and hills, walking and riding, or took my books into the copses at the edge of our land. Sasie came over to help us settle in, and my father had installed a groom in a room next to the stables. He was a very old man with a strange and mysterious past, for he claimed to be the bastard son of a nobleman. His manner of speaking held rudiments of nobility so he was probably telling the truth. He told the village tradesmen that he had served several generations of my father's family and had endless tales about horses he had trained. He had been fiercely mauled by a stallion and most of his stomach was missing or patched up; it was amazing that he was still able to ride and manage the stable.

Cranleigh at that time was a country village with a few roads of villas built for the richer tradesmen, and the 'big' houses round about. Many army and naval officers had retired into pretty houses with leafy gardens round the large green or in some of the roads near the borders of the village. My father's reputation must have preceded us, for only one or two people called.

That first summer in our house, Hilliards, soon showed that my mother's plan to change my father and make him settle down was not going to work. He drank as much as ever and started spending nights away from home, as his relationship with Frankie became more absorbing. Strangely, my mother often asked her to stay the night, and seemed to be encouraging a *ménage à trois*. As for myself, I could only watch what I was unable to understand, and tried with all my capability to bring peace to the chaos which was always breaking out. I soothed my father when he came home drunk and helped him to get to bed in the spare room when he needed my help. One day in desperation I told him to try and pull himself together and take on some responsibility. He hit me hard on the side of my head. At the same time he was treating me as a woman, in a way that I could not understand.

Later that term my father and mother took Frankie away with them on a caravan holiday in Cornwall. I cannot imagine what its purpose was, but the result was disastrous. My father, at the end of his tether, attacked my mother, and she had a great bruise over her eye which slightly damaged her sight. From this point our home life became impossible. I must have been very innocent of the ways of the world, for when my mother told me that Frankie was taking my father away from us I felt it as a great blow, for she had never been anything but gentle and kind to me. I was very torn emotionally as my mother expected me to treat her as a bad and despicable person.

The tragedy of non-understanding between my parents led me too into a period of tension which was almost insupportable. Even today, looking back on that time, I find their whole tormented relationship impossible to disentangle in my mind. As a fifteen year old I could only lie awake listening to their quarrels by night and continue to try to help them understand each other, not realising that at this stage it would be impossible. The pace at which everything was happening and sheer emotional exhaustion inhibited my pity for those two suffering people, which I was only able to feel, and in the case of my mother express, later on.

After sleepless nights I would go to school in a dazed state and sometimes had such severe headaches that my mother kept me at home – to the open envy of my schoolmates who knew nothing about my trouble and wished that they could have had the day off for something as trivial as a headache.

One day I arrived at school in such a condition of shock that the matron put me to bed in a quiet dormitory, and after that I became a weekly boarder. Soon after this my father left home and my mother took the necessary steps towards divorce. It was fortunate that Pat was still a boarder at his Hampton prep. school and that although the divorce of his parents affected him deeply, he missed the day-by-day strain.

The very ordinariness of school was a comfort to me. As the time for my homework was limited I was not tempted to overwork and as a boarder I was able to sing in the chapel choir. Daily evensong was before our supper. The choir mistress, a stern perfectionist, trained us to sing plainsong and I found great solace in its peace and purity. At weekends we were allowed walks in the wooded countryside. There was an austerity about our everyday life which would astonish present day pupils; we spent our leisure in our bare form room furnished only with worn desks and hard chairs, and at weekends were allowed a fire in the grate. As it was autumn we sat round it and roasted chestnuts that we had gathered in our walks through the woods.

Every alternate weekend I spent at home with my mother. These times were sad and difficult for us both. I became exhausted by her continuous condemnation of my father. On the face of things he was so clearly the wrongdoer, but my love for him and a feeling of loyalty prevented me from satisfying her with outright and continuous condemnation to match hers. Young and confused though I was I felt that their relationship had been broken down by deep and unconscious misunderstandings which precluded blame or guilt. So I was unable to be of real comfort to my mother until her need to cast my father as an unredeemable villain lessened and she began a new and happier life. Each of these weekends at home left me with a sad sense of failure.

It was many years before I saw my father for short and very occasional meetings; not until I took my husband and three children to stay with him in the hotel at Lechlade which he bought after the war and managed with a friend. We formed a warm relationship with him, and his nature, as I then discovered it, and the regrets he expressed about his marriage to my mother, made me feel that my fifteen-year-old intuitions about him had not been entirely wrong.

9

S T CATHERINE'S was at that time weak academically, but it brought me enrichment. Music was very important, there were an unusual number of musical girls and we had a close connection with the Royal Academy of Music. The chapel music and choral singing was of a high standard and I attended classes for musical appreciation, where, for the first time, I learnt something of musical construction and composition and how to listen carefully and with understanding.

Amongst my friends Mary Shott, a serious and precise girl, played Bach brilliantly. I listened to her practising, squeezed into the small practice room illicitly. Mary, who was also a high class mathematician, was faced with the problem of what subject to study when she left school. She chose maths and later became a nun, and no doubt her music contributed richly to convent life. After my first year I learnt the piano with a new young teacher, Cay Scovell. She became a close friend and I had little difficulty in persuading her that it did more for my musical education if *she* played for *me*. She also had the imagination to teach me difficult works by Bach and

Chopin which I loved, rather than more easy pieces, so although I never became a fluent performer my love of music deepened.

Miss Ireland taught English and History from the fifth form upwards. We called her Tilly and this name suited her. A bright and lively woman nearing sixty, with soft, untidy white hair and dark eyes, her vivacity and enthusiasm came very near eccentricity. She wore unfashionably long skirts and seemed absent minded about her clothes, which never sat in the sort of way that one expected. She brought to both her subjects a spirit of hero worship and fanaticism. Poets and statesmen alike came to life; Gladstone or Dizzy, Canning or Castlereagh, one would have her total allegiance and the other would be cast as villain. Prince Hal in Henry IV was her beloved hero and she saw in the living Prince of Wales his reincarnation. All this made literature and history vivid.

Tilly was also partisan where her pupils were concerned: she valued openly those who responded to her enthusiasm, those who were inattentive or lukewarm were urged and berated but not in a way that was really hurtful. Her digressions left us far behind in the syllabus when the time for examinations came. The results were mediocre and in the year when we took Matriculation, I was the only pupil in the small sixth form who passed, by working out the odds carefully on the questions we were likely to be asked and revising accordingly. When I came to teach in my turn I remembered Tilly and how important it had been to have subjects brought alive. I realised that I had valued her lessons far beyond the more competent work of other mistresses, and tried to bring life to my own teaching.

Miss Nichols, 'Nick', who taught languages, became a life long friend; I was still too advanced in French and German to be anything but bored by the actual lessons, but I was appointed her 'water carrier', for in those days there was no running water in the staff bedrooms and senior girls brought small cans of hot water for hand washing before meals. Nick's bedroom was full of pictures of France and Switzerland, as she loved to travel and went abroad every holiday. She soon discovered my own passion for travel and it drew us together. A very nervous woman with a nose like Cyrano de Bergerac's, she was always kind and patient.

At this time my mother, recovering from the shock of her divorce, went for a short holiday in Kent, and I was able to show her in letters the sympathy that it was so difficult to make her accept when I was actually with her. She wrote telling me that at the guest house where she was staying she had met a couple, a Major and Mrs Parselle, and she and Mrs Parselle had arranged to take their children to Lausanne during the coming summer holidays. Tom Parselle was 16 and Bess 15.

Pat and I were delighted to be back in Lausanne in Sasie's house at the edge of the lake. The Parselles were staying in a nearby hotel. Lilly and Aunt Mitzi also arrived and we all met every day for swimming, tennis or excursions. Lausanne had a wonderful *plage* with an enormous slide into the lake. When you stood at the top holding your tray and waiting your turn, the slide curved away into nothing and the sparkling blue lake seemed miles below. It was here that I won my one and only medal for sport, as I managed to stay on my tray for longer than anyone else in a competition.

One of our coach trips took us to Chamonix, up a mountain opposite Mont Blanc, and I took snapshots with which to decorate my dressing table at school. We all got on harmoniously and life seemed to have assumed a happy normality. Bess, a hearty schoolgirl, became my friend and we promised to write to each other when we were back at school. Tom, a Royal Air Force cadet at Cranwell, dark, sporting and good looking, was not quite unaware of me, although I was a little young for him. During the following term letters arrived with the Cranwell crest on their envelopes. My RAF boyfriend brought me some prestige and I was delighted to correspond with such a pleasant young man. I answered, but cannot think now what I found in my day-to-day school life to write about.

Although my mother was ostracised in Cranleigh by any family that had social pretensions, she was gradually building up her new life, for she once again began to take an interest in clothes, invited a few friends down from London, and got to know a few local families who like ourselves were not accepted by Cranleigh society – mainly because of some trouble between husband and wife, or because they spoke with the wrong sort of accent.

I brought friends with me at weekends and our household settled down peacefully.

My English grandfather and aunts, who must have been in some dilemma as to how to best divide their loyalty between my father and my mother, began, now that things were clearer, to get in touch with us again. For the first time I got to know my father's second sister, my aunt Gladys, a widow with three children: Harold, Joey and Kate. She was rich, and would send her car and chauffeur to fetch me from school to spend the weekend with them in Amersham.

For the first time I experienced formal English country life. Changing for dinner into clothes laid out for me by the maid, being served by a butler, my cousins with their own schoolroom and a Hunt Ball were all new to me. Joey, born the same year as me, and Kate a few years younger, were both passionate riders. They owned horses of a class very different from the riding school hacks that I was used to, and before my first ride I was silently apprehensive. Joey, pretty, feminine and very well turned out, took me in charge. I was given a horse known for its bolting habits which even she could not rein in. 'If it starts to get away, turn it uphill' she said.

As soon as we were out in the rolling green countryside, this was what I had to do. I found the wild gallop exhilarating, and once the horse had exhausted its first fervour it became manageable. Kate, who was already at that time earning her nick name of Farmer, had stayed at home mucking out the stables. Harold, because of his status as eldest of the children and public school boy, was rather aloof from the schoolroom. Joey and Kate had lessons with a governess. She was a very nice woman, but I did not envy them.

School life for me passed very pleasantly. I was no nearer being able to join in the general cult for games which obsessed most schoolgirls of my generation, but I was discreet and accepted even by the most ardent sports lovers. Now, in the sixth form, we worked in less bare surroundings. Our dark brown table could almost have been found in a private house, and our chairs were spindle back. We were all longing to be grown up, sang the popular songs of our day, experimented with our hairstyles and put on as much makeup as we dared.

Greta Garbo was my great model and I began to grow my hair, much to the sorrow of my mother who liked to send me off to the hairdresser regularly for the standard crinkly permanent wave.

Our only chance of wearing clothes other than uniform came on Saturday evenings, when we changed into long party dresses and danced with each other and the staff, to a small school band. My mother was as good as ever at making me pretty dresses, and these and light silk stockings and pointed evening shoes made me feel part of that exciting world beyond the school into which we couldn't wait to emerge. It must now seem as if we were very easily pleased, but the clothes, the fashionable music and the dancing brought us colour and gaiety to which we responded.

During November of my last school year I was confirmed in our chapel. We had confirmation classes with the Vicar of Bramley, our Chaplain. He was a very nice but quite uninspired man and although I enjoyed the slight sense of festivity as the day approached, for we gave each other bright cards and small books, I was utterly unprepared for the feeling of peace and happiness which overcame me as I walked back to my seat after the Bishop had laid his hands on me. We went up two by two in alphabetical order, and strangely the girl who knelt next to me, Lillian Carlton, became a close friend much later on in my life and is the only one from those days with whom I am still closely in touch.

My mother came with Aunt Gladys, and I tried to explain the change that had quietly come over me. I was very sad that neither then nor later could I share with her the inner peace which I had found and which continued to be renewed whenever I took communion.

One of the effects of growing up was that the school buildings which had seemed so very large and confusing when I was a new girl gradually shrank around me until I and all my friends with me felt oppressed and imprisoned. Miss Symes suggested that I should stay on at school for another year after matriculation as she wanted me as a guinea pig for Higher Certificate, which the school had decided to introduce, but I had been promised a year in Vienna with Uncle Alfred and Aunt Mitzi, to prepare myself for university, and nothing would make me forgo that.

A foretaste of liberation came when I went up to
London with my mother to take Matriculation in the
London University Examination Schools in South
Kensington. She had bought me new clothes right down
to the skin and I felt delightfully grown up in a bra and
suspender belt and artificial silk petticoat instead of the
liberty bodice and Chilprufe I had worn until then.

We stayed in a boarding house recommended to us
by Miss Symes. It was here that her mother lived when
she was in England. Mrs Symes was a very formidable
lady, even more formidable than her two headmistress
daughters – for there was a second Miss Symes whose
school was in the north of England. Mrs Symes was
Rome correspondent to the Times, and spent much of her
time abroad. We stayed on for the weekend and it was an
interesting experience to see 'my' Miss Symes, such a
figure of power and authority, with her equally
dominating sister, sharing a table with their mother and
behaving like two schoolgirls out for a treat.

During the last weeks of the term we all indulged
ourselves in a certain degree of nostalgia. We swore life
long friendship and promised to meet regularly. When
the last week came we spent the evenings going to
mistresses' rooms, bearing small presents, to say our
goodbyes. My parting from Leila Bott was full of
confused feelings. Elation that at last friendships would
be untrammelled by school rules was mixed with a
sadness that my visits to her room where she had shown
me so much affection and kindness were to end. I knew

that the urge towards a larger life which I felt so strongly in myself would mean a change in our relationship, and that this future opening before me was more unpredictable than anything I had experienced before.

As a final exercise in nostalgia I went to the cinema in Guildford with four of my friends who were also leaving. This was strictly forbidden, but the film, *Young Woodley*, was the story of a public school sixth former who falls in love with his headmaster's wife and is expelled. It seemed singularly suited to our emotional mood, which mixed fun with self dramatisation.

When our last evening chapel came and traditionally those of us who were leaving were allowed to choose a hymn, we chose the one that had been sung in young Woodley's chapel at the sad conclusion of his story: 'Time like an everlasting stream bears all its sons away, they fly forgotten as a dream flies at the opening day'. Bathed in a mixture of pathos, exhilaration and the real sadness of parting for unknown futures, we filed out of chapel. One more night in the dormitory and our life together was over.

Feeling beautifully free I came home. I was only sixteen and life stretched ahead of me full of happy possibilities. I longed for the autumn and Vienna, but in the meanwhile we were to have a holiday in Wales with the Parselles.

My mother and Anne Parselle had rented a small house at Rhos-on-Sea. Pat must have felt a bit left out because Bess had also left school, and Tom, in his second year at Cranwell, considered himself a man of the world. We bathed in the rough and rocky sea and Bess and I changed elegantly into fashionable beach pyjamas in spite of the cold and wind. We smoked cigarettes from long holders; I had succeeded in growing my hair to the length of Garbo's and wore it straight and tucked behind my ears as she did, and Tom and I fell in love.

I did not suddenly plunge into ecstasy but we wandered out for walks after dark, held hands, kissed, went to local dances and everything was very poignant. Tom, half Irish, had a delightfully wistful and caressing way of talking to me and he punctuated his romantic talk with descriptions of his fellow cadets being scraped off aeroplanes and motorcycles that they had crashed. I was both very happy and very sad; I realised how young we both were, and that we must soon part. There was a dreaminess and unreality about the holiday as it did not occur to me to forgo my stay in Vienna. The Welsh landscape – mountains and the sea together, which I had never experienced before – made a suitable backcloth and the ruined castles on the hillsides moved me to poetry.

When Tom's leave came to an end and he returned to Cranwell I missed him greatly, shut myself in my room, read the poems of Keats that he had left behind with me, and pored over letters that came almost every day.

After we had returned to Cranleigh, he came to stay for a week. We went for walks, took photos and tried to comfort each other about our coming parting. Before he left he gave me a golden RAF brooch which I wore proudly.

My mother took me to buy clothes for the winter: my first 'grownup' dresses and a lamb 'fur' coat. The two dresses were of hyacinth blue and of very dark green woollen material and both had fashionable white revers. Aunt Gladys met me in London to buy me an evening dress as a reward for my good examination results. We chose a very lacy affair in a pastel brown/pink. It had a full skirt and tight bodice, with a flower at the waist. Entirely her taste, it didn't accord at all with my image of myself; I looked a typical 'English Rose', but I could not hurt her, so I fell in with her choice and thanked her affectionately.

It now turned out that my grandfather, who was to take me to Vienna, and I were to have a companion: Tanya Moiseiwitch, daughter of Benno Moiseiwitch and the violinist Daisy Kennedy, who had from the Hampton days asked me to parties in their house in London and were distant connections of my Austrian family.

At the end of the summer, on a platform at Victoria Station, surrounded by a large contingent of the Moiseiwitch family, I kissed my mother goodbye and set off in the boat train with my grandfather and Tanya.

Tanya was a tall, very slim girl with dark eyes and hair. Her face was a perfect oval, expressive in a way that reminded me of a ballerina. Her sleek hair was like a shining black cap and her eyes wore a melancholy expression. From the start we found that we shared many things and were drawn close in friendship.

My grandfather had decided to break the journey at Nuremberg. Tanya and I shared a small hotel room and settled down to writing – she in her diary and I a letter to Tom. Then we went on a coach trip round the town. I had stopped in Nuremberg several times before, but I saw the medieval houses and their Dürer-like frescoes on many of the outer walls with newly awakened eyes. The castle with its dungeon full of horrible instruments of torture and crude illustrations of how they had been used, froze me, but I already believed in accepting experiences as they came, even if they were hard to bear. In the evening we went to the opera and saw *The Student Prince*, which left little impression on me.

After another long train journey we arrived in Vienna. Uncle Alfred was on the platform to meet us, and almost instantly, and as it now seems symbolically, my hat, a perfect fit in England, was seized by the strong and perpetual Viennese wind, lifted off my head and flung bounding along the platform.

That was the last time I wore it.

10

I N MY AUNT and uncle's flat, the same one in which I spent four of my childhood years, I settled in the room that had been Willy's. It had a large desk, for I was to do a lot of work to prepare myself for Oxford. My mother had planned this for me and although eager to immerse myself in German literature. I knew too little about Oxford to know whether I wanted to go there.

In spite of my love of Vienna and the longing I felt to be back again, I became very conscious of my Englishness. My clothes which had seemed so stylish and sophisticated at home, I found to be well out of fashion. I wore the dresses self-consciously for a while but they were soon replaced by some handed over by Lilly and altered for me a by a visiting dressmaker. My fur coat, which I wore nonchalantly open at home, or clutched about with one hand, I soon gathered into a broad leather belt and Lilly gave me a small knitted skull cap to replace the flyaway hat.

I very much looked back over my shoulder at England. I missed my mother and Tom and wrote them long letters. Photographs of Tom and my St Catherine's friends were on the bookcases and indeed everywhere there was room for them.

I was not quite seventeen but had come over thinking myself grown up; now I found myself treated in many ways as a child. I only discovered gradually how unsophisticated I was compared to the young Viennese and could not understand why, when I was accepted by Tom and his friends who were older than the boys in the circle in which I found myself, it was hard to adjust myself. I did not realise that I was not as overtly sexual as the girls of my age. I wanted to get to know people and talk to them, to share my interests, but that was not what was needed.

Society, after the fall of the Austro-Hungarian empire had become very permissive and Vienna was economically like a head without a body. As a result few could afford early marriage and I soon found that Lilly, Willy and their friends had lovers and went with them on many weekend excursions and holidays. Lilly was going about with Fritz Huttrer, who she eventually married, and Willy was carrying on affairs with several girls. His serious love at that time was a princess of the Imperial family and she returned his love. Sadly there seemed for them no possible future together since he, a commoner and a Jew, would have been considered quite unsuitable as her husband. Her father, after an interview with Uncle Alfred, sent her away to Belgium and Willy consoled himself with other girls.

Tanya, even less sophisticated than I was, wore a tartan kilt and plain jumper and was astonished but unperturbed that her fourteen-year-old cousin used heavy makeup, dressed as if she were twenty and went out regularly with boys much older than herself. I was together with Tanya almost every day. Her mother had parted from Benno Moiseiwitch and married the poet John Drinkwater and she moved at home amongst a circle of musicians, poets and playwrights. My friendship with her during these first months in Vienna brought me for the first time close to someone with a deep love of all the arts.

We went together to art galleries, plays and concerts and I copied her by keeping a scrap book into which I stuck newspaper cuttings, postcards and tickets etc., as a kind of diary. This began with reviews from the *Observer*, pictures of film stars and accounts of Tom's success on the track and rugby field. Gradually they changed to programmes of Viennese plays, reviews of Austrian books, and tickets from concerts and dances. In November Daisy Kennedy came over to give a recital and to take Tanya home with her. After that we wrote each other long letters, hers often covered more than ten pages.

Meanwhile I had become deeply immersed in German literature. My elderly teacher came twice a week and gave me an introduction to Goethe and Schiller and the many writers who were their contemporaries. Soon I was reading avidly. I also discovered that a ticket for the

Burgtheater, the Viennese state theatre, was cheaper than entrance to a cinema at home. So I went to all performances of classical plays. I read French plays with a French woman, but these did not move me nearly as much; Corneille struck me as too rigid and courtly, Molière too mannered, and it was only many years later, following a performance of *Phèdre*, that I grew to understand the passion of Racine. My teacher had a boring and literal mind and I was still young enough to be affected by the attitude of the person with whom I was working.

I soon discovered that Aunt Mitzi seemed to trust me to come and go as I pleased, provided that I told her if I was going out for a meal. I spent many hours writing essays and soon began to write both poetry and prose for my own pleasure. But in the evening, when I became tired of sitting at my desk, I would walk out into the frosty Viennese night and explore the streets of the old town. I lost myself in the sharply contrasting narrow dark side streets beneath the looming pinnacles of the cathedral, where prostitutes lurked in arched doorways, and the brightly lit fashionable shopping streets. I deeply enjoyed the freedom and solitude I was discovering in this way.

I could not enjoy music as I did the theatre. Tickets for concerts and particularly for the Opera were far more expensive and I depended on invitations. In addition to recitals by Daisy Kennedy and Benno Moiseiwitch, to which I was given complimentary tickets, Aunt Mitzi took me to *The Messiah* with Furtwängler conducting, and to an expressive performance of Beethoven's Ninth. Since my mother did not particularly enjoy concerts my experience of performed music had been very limited and I was little prepared for the great enjoyment it brought me.

At this time Uncle Alfred's eldest brother, a musician and critic, came to Vienna to be at the bedside of their mother who was dying of cancer. She was in a nursing home and one afternoon when I myself went to visit her I encountered Rudolf. We both had to await our turn to see her and in the waiting room he quizzed me about my knowledge of music. When he discovered that I had been in the school choir he gave me various tests which included, as I remember, singing an augmented seventh. On my succeeding in this, he invited me to go with him to the opera.

It was to *Siegfried* that we went and we sat in one of the front rows of the stalls. With the libretto between us he made me follow it moment by moment. I enjoyed the sense of occasion, the attention of someone so mature and distinguished, and the opera itself brought me some pleasure, but I still could not yield to the convention. The plot, which differed so much from the literary tradition on which were based the films which had beguiled me in Baden, I found disappointing. Nor was I unconscious of the absurdities which seemed an inevitable part of all operas: Siegfried was a handsome and athletic man without the then customary singer's paunch; he leapt and bounded over rocks and logs, but his voice was mediocre. Brunhild, when at long last she was revealed asleep on her rock, was almost as large as the rock itself. Her voice however was superb. This was the only visit that I paid to the Vienna Opera House during my stay.

My love for the theatre deepened and became an integral part of my life. I became profoundly absorbed by the beautiful and intricate complexes of human emotions that I found there, and filled with wonder at their orchestration. It affected my reading and greatly deepened my experience of life. I came to prefer an evening at the Burgtheater by myself to the social gatherings of my age group. I was very happy and very serious.

At first when I came to Vienna I went regularly to communion at the English church just down the road. One day, during the months before Christmas, I was invited to lunch by one of my mother's cousins. He was married to a young American opera singer. Their flat, decorated in the bold decor of the thirties, impressed me very much. The centre of it was a studio designed in black and red. The carpet was red, the grand piano, chair and bookshelves black, and everywhere in the flat were books which I inspected eagerly. This eagerness must have pleased my cousins for they listened kindly to me enthusiastic ideas and I came away with a newly published history of philosophy.

As I read this book the Christian dogma that I had absorbed at school fell away and I seemed to be moving into a world filled with deep and wide freedom. I experienced an elation which is usually connected with conversion into, and not out of, religion, and I received a God's eye view of a universe of cause and effect where to understand all would be to know all and where, if it were possible to comprehend its vast workings, everything would seem to be in exactly the right place. I happily shed religious habits which I now felt so narrow and restricting and moved forward into this new freedom.

Christmas was nearing and I spent a lot of time hunting round the shops for presents to send home to my friends and family. Delighted, I found a small book of Shelley's poems for Tanya. With everything posted I waited eagerly for letters and parcels for me. Snow came and the soft white roofs and clean fresh air carried me away from my growing world of arts and philosophy into the magic Vienna of my childhood.

Uncle Alfred was a stern and unbending atheist and ignored Christmas completely. Lilly and Willy were away skiing with a party of their friends and Aunt Mitzi was glad to have me to share with her what would otherwise have been a very bleak Christmas. I waited vainly for post from home; right up to Christmas Eve nothing had come. In the evening Aunt Mitzi called me into the drawing room where she had decorated a small Christmas tree and there on a table were all my parcels and letters which she had kept secret from me. From my mother, I found a much longed for collection of Rupert Brooke's poems, from Tom a richly bound Omar

Khayyam and from Tanya a signed copy of poems by
John Drinkwater. There too were letters and cards from
all my friends.

I drew very close to Aunt Mitzi during my stay with
her and gradually gained insight into her lonely life.
Uncle Alfred was affectionate with me but cool with his
own family. Lilly, affected by the coldness in the family,
spoke little more to her parents than was absolutely
necessary and went her own way. Willy was kind,
humorous and good natured with us all.

Aunt Irene and Uncle Edmund still lived in my
grandmother's flat. Uncle Edmund had a large library
and was happy to lend me books. He was immensely
well read but to his sorrow his natural laziness kept him
from any achievement of the intellect. Unlike his sisters,
there was nothing creative in his character.

Aunt Otti Fluss and Lily Zingarelli I saw often and
there was little Carla and another small Fluss cousin with
whom I enjoyed playing, for I still loved the company of
children. One of Aunt Irene's twin daughters came on a
visit from Poland. Aunt Carla was not as smart and
beautiful as her sister Magda but we became close and I
visited her and went out with her. Her husband owned a
restaurant in Warsaw and I have always been sorry that I
wasn't able to visit them there when it still would have
been a possibility. She had a young son called Peter and
was one of the few of my mother's cousins who was
happy in her marriage.

Gradually some of my childhood friends started coming back into my life. Mausi, the closest and dearest of them rang me up and invited me to go to a dance with her and some boys. She had grown into a beautiful young woman, much older looking and more sophisticated than I was.

It soon appeared that the young men of our group had no intention of having more than an occasional dance with the simple English girl she had foisted on them. Mausi and her swains left me as soon as we entered the ballroom and I was alone in my English Rose dress not knowing what had gone wrong. So came about the end of a long friendship. Girl friends were obviously quite unimportant in Mausi's life. My sadness at the loss of a friend was balanced by the anger I felt at the way I had been treated; in England I would not have been left to languish as a wallflower, I comforted myself.

Very happily for me there was someone whose friendship had stronger roots: Max Perutz was a keen photographer and was in the habit of coming most days after school to use the darkroom which had been arranged in the upper floor of our flat. He always looked for me and soon enlisted me as his assistant and taught me how to develop prints and make enlargements. If I was busy reading or writing an essay he would bring me some prints which needed retouching into the room where I was working and drove me frantic by squealing a sharp knife point over a surface that needed lightening.

He was a highly intelligent boy, a pupil at the Theresianum – the former military academy – which was now a high status boarding school, and we soon found many interests to share. His true Austrian sense of humour accorded well with my English one and he teased me gently when I was too earnest and took my vocation as a writer too seriously. Our friendship grew naturally and affectionately.

His photographs were almost all of his beloved mountains and of a very high standard, some being accepted for publication in periodicals. He was a passionate skier and a skilled and responsible rock climber. I could not follow him there but we went out often together into the Vienna Woods and to restaurants and cafés, films, plays and light operas. I often too went to his parents' flat and shared his meals when the rest of the family were out.

In time other friends came and other boys took me out on occasions, but it was Max's affectionate friendship which brought me companionship and humour and saved me from the danger of over-precociousness and over-absorption in my inner life.

Shortly before Christmas someone who was to influence my life profoundly came to Vienna. Aunt Toni's husband Rudolf von Kahler had died and Erich, their only son, arrived to help her with the division of her house into two flats, to sort out the enormous library and settle her into her new life on the ground floor.

I had often visited Aunt Toni in her house in its garden in the Cottage and met some of the artists and writers who were her friends. For many years she suffered from a heart complaint and Uncle Rudolf took such care of her that he would not allow her to go beyond the house and garden except for rare shopping trips in a cab. She still showed the lively original character of her youth, attracted interesting people around her, read widely, and when Erich was a schoolboy had shared his Latin and Greek lessons. Now she began to paint.

Pepi Willenski, the throat specialist who had operated in my tonsils, was a considerable artist and only too willing to teach her, but asserting her will she developed her own technique. She would not mix paints and her palette was covered with small ovals of pure colours. The pictures she painted were of vases of flowers, original and primitively charming.

I had only met Erich once before, when we broke a journey by a few days in Wolfratshausen near Munich. He was a solid man with a fine head, his eyes were short sighted behind thick glasses and his slightly protruding jaw gave him a Hapsburg look. He soon began to take a great interest in me, read my poems, listened to my ideas, influenced my reading and drew me into his circle of friends. He had no children of his own and my mother was his favourite cousin.

The expansion of my mind and whole range of experience was tremendously exciting. Although he teased me by calling me 'child' he treated me as an adult. His mind encompassed a culture which included the whole of Europe. This was brought home to me when at a party he gave, the word was passed round: 'Lawrence is dead'. In spite of my interest in literature, no one in England had ever mentioned D.H. Lawrence to me. Kindly, they explained his importance. It was through Erich too that I first came to hear of Virginia Woolf.

Never have I had the truth of the Chinese saying 'When the pupil is ready, the teacher appears' proved to me more clearly. Now I was to have not one but many teachers. It was through Aunt Toni that I met Aunt Toni's cousin the poet and playwright Richard Beer-Hofmann, who had been one of a famous trio of Viennese writers together with Arthur Schnitzler and Hugo von Hoffmannstal. Although his literary reputation is distinguished, his poems published in anthologies and his plays acted, his opus is small. He was a slow writer much given to polishing and re-polishing. Even his famous drama trilogy Jacob's Dream goes no further than the prologue and the first play.

A great part of his creative genius must have been channelled into his living. As a young man he had fallen romantically in love with a beautiful sixteen year old he had found serving behind the counter of one of the famous Viennese confectioners. He married her, she was as good as she was beautiful and when I met them, both in their seventies, they appeared just as much in love as ever. He travelled to all the most famous places in Europe to find settings for her, collected clothes and jewellery to adorn her, and rare antiques for their home. Paula remained quite unspoiled. They had three children: Gabriel, Miriam and Naema. Sadly he regarded them too merely as ornaments fitting for Paula, she had love mainly for him, and the children were always on the outside of this close marriage.

Richard, a writer of my own blood, wise, witty and charming, immediately won my admiration and devotion. I saw him regularly, mostly in Erich's company, and he never treated me as the young, hero worshipping, inexperienced girl that I was. He gave me copies of his book inscribed with wise words and trinkets from among his treasures. Paula encouraged me with love from her warm and simple heart, seeing in me perhaps the grandchild she was never to have.

At some time after Christmas Erich's wife Fine (Josefine) came to Vienna. Although they shared their Wolfratshausen home and large circle of friends, it was a very free marriage. Both of them had a series of lovers, and Fine had had a long lasting affair with the famous Heidelberg Professor of German Literature and author of many books of biography and criticism, Friedrich Gundolf. She was a dark eyed passionate woman with a masculine incisiveness of intellect, and like Erich she 'adopted' me and I grew fond of her.

Amongst Erich's friends was the writer and philosopher Rudolf Kassner. He asked me to tea in his house and at the recommendation of Erich, read my poems. He praised them and compared them to Lawrence's. I had not at that time read anything by Lawrence so it could not have been a direct influence. I must have picked my style 'out of the air'. Kassner, crippled from birth, had a body normal as far as his legs, which were stunted and short and he walked laboriously with two special metal sticks. He told me how when he was a schoolboy he had found it difficult to carry the many heavy books and solved the problem by taking them apart and carrying only the necessary pages. This was then copied by all his class and became an elegant fashion in his school.

It was not only living people who had a deep effect on me. My imagination was inhabited by the lives and personalities of dead writers and artists and I felt a close companionship to them. Strangely it was a dead actor who became a symbol for that life of the spirit which so drew me. Joseph Kainz had died at close on fifty in the years before the First World War. He was to the German speaking theatre what Nijinsky had been to ballet. His parents had been quite simple people, he had had little education but like Nijinsky had an innate and deep understanding for roles which it otherwise would have been quite beyond his mental capacity to understand.

My mother, who had seen him in her youth, could not describe what his spell binding consisted of, nor in what way he differed from the actors I myself saw and admired. His aura lived on and when I hunted out a photograph of him from old newspaper files I found even here an echo of his strange power and an unusual identity with the character of Hamlet in which he was depicted.

After the New Year I was asked by a girl who had several times invited me to parties, whether I would join her and an English friend who was staying with her, on a short skiing holiday. I was eager to take this first chance that had come my way of learning a sport to which all the other young people I knew were dedicated.

Lilly fitted me out with old clothes of hers and a pair of skis and with a borrowed rucksack on my back I was taken to join the party at the station. The holiday was organised through *Kraft durch Freude* (Strength through Joy) and was part of the cult which had on its shadow side the glorification of the 'Aryan' race and the persecution of the Jews. I cannot understand the readiness with which I was encouraged to join such a group and can only suppose that the full menace of Nazi ideas had not yet become clear. As far as I can remember they were treated by my friends with derision.

The holiday was very cheap and we travelled overnight on the milk train which involved being shunted into a siding at midnight to wait for four hours for the milk which we were to deliver. The third class carriages in which we travelled had solid wooden benches back to back, with the luggage racks joining them. I managed to get some sleep on one of these racks where, with my rucksack as a pillow, I could at least stretch my legs. In the very early morning we left the stuffy train and breathed clear cold air from the snow covered mountains. We slung our skis and baggage onto a bus on skids which drove us up to a youth hostel in one of the high valleys of the Radstädter Tauern. It was off the road which led over the pass to Italy which Goethe had traversed in his coach, eager and impatient for the Classical world.

The hostel was a large very simply furnished wooden house and we slept in dormitories and ate at long wooden tables. The skiing was strenuous – there were no ski lifts and we walked uphill with strips of sealskin strapped to our skis. Never an athlete, I grew very tired but nothing could spoil my joy in the mountains. I never loved the winter mountains as I did the summer ones, their frozen white beauty concealed so much subtle variety, but the quietness and purity, the feather like shapes of the trees, the deep blue sky and sunshine in which we could lounge with bare arms on benches which we had dug for ourselves in the snow and covered with rugs, brought great enjoyment.

In spite of the loveliness there was one day when the mountains showed their menace: we were practising on a small steep slope when the next slope, which in formation was exactly the same as ours, loosened and crumbled into a great heap of snow in the valley. It was an avalanche! As it moved – not from top to bottom, but the whole slope at once – it was accompanied by a strangely muted rumbling.

The young people we were with were good natured and cheerful – there was a lot of singing and fumbling in the dark which I avoided as far as I could without being hurtful. It was amongst these young Austrians that I experienced Nazi talk for the first time. They used the word 'Jew' as a sneering epithet when they talked about sportsmen or actors. I did not hide the fact that my family were Jewish, though I didn't want to embarrass my friend – who though not Jewish herself did not entertain Nazis in her house – by being over aggressive.

I discovered then as later that those young people who had been indoctrinated by Nazi ideology were ambivalent and quite impervious to truth. They could not absorb the fact that I, English and 'Aryan' looking, who they liked and treated kindly, was half Jewish. There was a confusing unreality about their states of mind and I could not help feeling that when they were a little older they would become more clear sighted and consistent. It seemed impossible to detect a real spirit of evil at work among those cheerful young people.

When I arrived back in Vienna sunburnt and exhausted I found my mother there. She had come for a short visit. I was very happy to see her again and had the strange experience of speaking German better than she did. Although her accent was perfect I noticed that many expressions she used were direct translations from English.

Strangely, she was very shocked indeed when I told her that I no longer went to church or believed in God. I could not understand why she should mind when she herself had no belief and I had always had to go to church alone. We had a heated argument as I tried to inspire her with my new and fascinating vision of the world. I could not succeed, but apart from this one scene we enjoyed our reunion. Vienna was a very happy place for us.

11

WINTER had not quite moved into the quick Viennese spring when a niece of Uncle Alfred came to stay. She was a daughter of the third of the three brothers – Hans Teller, the only one of them who still lived in Prague where they had all been born and where he still managed the family business, a factory for the processing of sugar beet.

Mimsch, who had at this time been married for several years, was fair, slim and elegant. She was very gifted and painted lively water colours, drew fine portraits, played the piano fluently and tennis with brightness and ease. Possibly because there were too many of these gifts, or perhaps because she always had more than sufficient money to live a comfortable life surrounded by beautiful things, she treated her gifts lightly and used them only for pleasure and occasional pocket money. She took a liking to me and invited me to follow her to Prague.

I had for some time wished that I could visit some of the countries which were so near to Austria but far from

England. Particularly Italy and Hungary drew me strongly. I had resigned myself to saving too little money to allow myself to travel. I spent sparingly on myself – my clothes were hand downs from Lilly and I walked everywhere to save tram fares, so that I could afford my tickets to the Burgtheater. Prague had been described to me as a lovely city and I was delighted when my mother pressed me to accept the invitation.

The train journey passed through Brno and I gazed through the window to see what I could of this birthplace of Grossmama and her sisters and brother. The citadel on its rock surrounded by dark forests are in my memory, a setting for the many stories of their childhood told to me by Grossmama and Aunt Toni.

Mimsch and her husband Heinz, a small, neat, fair man, met me at Prague station and drove me to their comfortable flat. There were not many rooms but all was bright and comfortable. Pictures painted by Mimsch hung on the walls, and the furniture, ornaments and textiles echoed their bright colours, space and light.

Every day of my stay we went out. Prague was full of dark mysterious streets in the old town on the nearer side of the river. I found myself in the middle ages and was particularly moved by the Jewish quarter with its small gothic synagogue where the vaulting instead of being crossed, had a fifth rib.[9] By the headstones in the ancient

---

[9] The builders were not allowed to incorporate the sign of the cross into a synagogue.

cemetery were piles of pebbles added one by one by mourners and visitors through the centuries. I felt a great sadness for the Jewish people so deeply rooted in the history of these ancient towns yet ever and again so cruelly treated, for the story of Prague included many persecutions.

A wide bridge led over the Moldau and we passed the life-size gilded statue of King Wenceslas on our way to the Hradčany, Prague's splendid citadel. The cathedral and staterooms were partly ornate baroque, and we saw the window from which the Catholic lords had been hurled to what might have been their death, had not an opportunely sited muck heap broken their fall. In the shadow of the castle stood a row of alchemists' houses like medieval dolls' houses, in a deserted cobbled street.[10] On this side of the river there were many elegant houses with gardens, green now with fresh spring leaves.

For the first time I met Mimsch's parents and her sister Nusschi, younger than her and overshadowed by her brilliance. Painfully reserved, she preferred the company of animals to human beings.

Heinz and Mimsch were both keen golfers and as they didn't wish to miss their weekly round they took me with them to the course in the country outside Prague. There they handed me over to the English professional to give me a lesson. I had never before been the slightest bit

---

[10] Deserted no more: Golden Lane, one of the most popular tourist attractions in Prague.

interested in golf but there, in the spring countryside, I became eager for yet another new experience. The pro, pleased to be with an English girl, was cheerful and encouraging and I did quite well – probably better than I ever did again. It gave me a taste for golf and showed me that I could do well enough, and later, back in England, I enjoyed many friendly foursomes in this game where less than in any other does one spoil the pleasure of those who play better.

Mimsch and I became quite intimate and one day she asked me if I was looking forward to having children. Without hesitation I said 'yes' and she told me that she had had several abortions. This seemed to me very sad. Later, when she and Heinz came to England as refugees she had two pretty daughters who had inherited her charm and some of her gifts. She sent me home with several of her dresses, which under the eye of Aunt Mitzi were altered so that they were indistinguishable from the spring fashions in the shops.

In Vienna the quick spring had passed into summer, which was both enervating and intoxicating. The hot air beat through open windows and the distant muffled pulsing of the traffic came to me as I worked, read or just day dreamed.

One day I was told that Uncle Alfred and Aunt Mitzi were going to sell their flat and move into a smaller, cheaper one nearer the centre of town. There would be no room for me and they had arranged for me to stay with Aunt Toni. At first I felt sad – I had come to feel I was a member of the family, but after a period of living with Aunt Toni and commuting to and fro for my lessons, I began to settle down and enjoy my small room and the garden with its romantic air of being a forgotten corner of a park, with large trees, heavy bushes and straying flowers.

Aunt Mitzi and Uncle Alfred's flat was dark and restricted and I always came away from visits with a feeling of gloom. In truth their married life changed here to tragedy and I was to witness the opening stages. For Uncle Alfred, ascetic and taciturn, was beginning to see a great deal of Fine Kahler. He, whose marriage had been 'on the rebound' and who had never been able to show physical affection except to his mother and to near-children like myself, was being taught late in life what warmth with a woman could be.

I do not know how far love in any sense in which I would then have accepted it was involved, for Fine had had many similar relationships. Erich looked on benignly and was pleased that a richness of experience was being offered to Uncle Alfred. Aunt Mitzi's melancholy deepened and two years later she made an attempt at suicide. This drew no kindness from Uncle Alfred who was quite unable to awaken any feeling towards her other than a dogged sense of duty, and their marriage lapsed into almost complete silence.

But in that hot June, unaware of the tragedy that was building up, Alfred and Fine's relationship was to me one more manifestation of the richness of life. Erich had invited a young protégé of his to come to Vienna that summer to help with the sorting out of his father's library. Erich Aaron was a tall, sallow, young Jew with a long melancholy brown face and bushy hair. He was in his late twenties, very serious and working on an anthology of aphorisms and quotations mainly from the classics. To avoid the confusion of having two Erichs about, he was always called Syl, for his birthday was on New Year's Eve, the feast of Saint Sylvester. It was now decided that I should stop my lessons with the old professor and learn with Syl instead.

It is to Syl that I owe my first introduction to many of the Romantic and more modern German poets. I have in particular a memory of sitting on a hill in the Vienna Woods with him, the country and town spread below us in a summer haze, reading for the first time poems from Rilke's *Buch der Bilder*. It is a gentle and happy memory. Poor Syl was too meek and unworldly to survive the calamities which were to come so soon. Even though, with the Kahlers' help, he escaped from Germany to Italy, he drowned himself in the Italian sea.

Max came often that hot summer and lured me away from my romantic musings to picnics in the country, or swimming in one of the many outdoor pools. Patiently he taught me how to dive – another lasting pleasure which I acquired at that time. On some days we went swimming in the wide strong Danube. The current was so swift that we started by walking a long distance upstream from the beach where we had changed. Then we would swim straight out to midstream and turn at once towards the bank. The timing had to be exact, for otherwise we would have been carried far beyond the point at which we needed to come ashore.

Max was a keen canoeist and one day we took a picnic and went far into the maze of wooded swamps which edge the Danube downstream from Vienna. We seemed to be lost in a land of strange trees, black mud, frogs and unexpected birds. I cannot remember how we managed to emerge again into the mainstream from those many sluggish streams which all looked alike.

Other boys called to take me swimming and one of them was a quiet eighteen year old who I had got to know at the Consular Academy where I went twice a week for Spanish lessons. This boy had made a habit of walking some of the way home with me. He was a widow's son and talked to me about life with his mother and how he wasn't ashamed to help with women's tasks like washing up and mending. He wore the Nazi swastika in his lapel and I was confronted once more by the dismaying split mind of the fanatic: on the one side was his gently considerate nature, on the other a total and literal belief in Nazi dogma. Again I found that the admission that I had Jewish blood could not be accepted realistically. He found me likeable and even lovable but a Jew was to him some sort of fabulous monster in no way connected with the real world to which I belonged. When I left Vienna he gave me his photo and asked me to write to him.

As the summer months passed, my life seemed to reach a climax of joy and richness. So much of it was spent out of doors; sitting in the cool garden reading, or on vine-laced terraces with Erich and Richard, drinking the new wine and eating curd cheese flavoured with bright little piles of chives, mustard and paprika heaped on the side of my plate. We drove into the country for walks and meals in taverns in the villages.

Sometimes outings took me into the Wachau, that legendary part of the Danube where it narrows between wooded precipices. Here small towns clustered round castles of medieval robber barons who used to stretch a chain across the narrows and plunder ships. My favourite castle was Dürnstein, for here the minstrel Blondel after singing a song composed by himself and his king Richard I of England[11] outside half the castles of Europe, was at last answered by his friend's voice.

During this summer Richard Beer-Hofmann produced Parts One and Two of Goethe's *Faust* for the Burgtheater, to be shown for the first time in history as one long performance. We were given a box for the opening night, a sparkling occasion with all the elegant world of Viennese society and intelligentsia present. Lilly Strakosch, daughter of the husband of my dead great aunt Rosa by his second marriage, became a close friend of mine. Soon to become engaged to Heinz Schitzler, son

---

[11] Richard the Lionheart.

of Arthur, who was producing interesting modern plays in the Theater in der Josefstadt, she shared my love of the theatre. Her father Siegfried entertained actors, writers and opera singers in his house and I felt yet nearer to the heart of Vienna's artistic life.

I became very close to Aunt Toni and I believe she enjoyed having me with her. Through the idleness that Uncle Rudolf had forced upon her she had become fat and comfortable looking and moved about the flat slowly. Her voice was even and lazy but that was deceptive, for she was a very acute observer and her remarks often carried a trace of half humorous malice which one could never quite believe in, coming from the mouth of one so phlegmatic.

We had living with us her companion/nurse Anne-Marie, a racy woman of about forty with a strong Berlin accent. She had a dry humour and a steady man friend who she referred to as her 'Grandmother'. We shared little harmless plots and plans to circumvent some of Aunt Toni's obstinacies. The chief of these lay in her refusal to change Rudolf's custom of having the house completely shuttered and barred at night. The heat of the summer rose to a peak when the thermometer stood at over seventy night and day and we had to use our utmost cunning to bring enough air into the flat to prevent our dying of heat stroke.

So that bright summer moved towards the end of my stay in Vienna. Happily I would have spent the rest of my life there, for I had found a richness, a sense of belonging, a coming into my heritage which I was loath to leave. My life had been a series of clearly divided chapters and I was reaching the close of yet another one. But I was still very young and with a strong appetite for the future, and fortunately had no premonition how long it would be before I came to Vienna again, and that when I did the whole of life as I had known it would have been swept away, and my family scattered.

12

ALTHOUGH my stay in Vienna had nearly come to an end I was not yet to leave Austria, for Max had invited me to stay with him in his parents' house in the mountains. Reichenau, only a few hours by train from Vienna, was a prosperous resort where many Viennese had their country villas. It is in a rich green valley surrounded by mountains, the greatest of which is the Rax.

Uncle Alfred had designed the Perutz's villa, large, with all modern conveniences. For the first time I tasted food from a refrigerator – fresh raspberries, strawberries and tomatoes picked from their own large garden. It was still a very hot summer and the refreshing taste of cold fruit is vivid in my memory.

Friends of Max's parents and of his sister and brother filled the house, coming and going, but Max and I led our own life, taking care to be punctual for meals.

A great deal of our time was spent at the swimming pool set in a hollow in the woods, where the mountains towered above us. The cult of sunbathing was at its height and, hating to be different from any of the other young people, I took no precautions to protect my very fair skin. The result was severe burns and blisters and a night of pain and feverish dreams. It took me many years to capitulate and sit in the shade, which I thought was only for the middle aged and old.

Max, determined to train me as a passable mountaineer, had started our first excursion by waking me early so that we could put two hours of uphill climbing behind us before we paused for breakfast. We soon discovered that walking without eating first was not for me – I had to be resuscitated with a sandwich before the first half hour had passed. Max proved himself to be an excellent guide, for he set a slow, measured pace which I could follow easily and I acquitted myself well enough for him to start planning more ambitiously.

The Rax as well as being an imposingly dramatic mountain presented a series of climbs which could be graded technically from the most simple to the most advanced. Max decided to take me on a climb which included in a small way every problem which a true rock climber had to face. Since Mr and Mrs Perutz would have felt too responsible to my mother to have given their permission, we decided to plan in secret. The best way of carrying out what we had in mind, Max said, would be to go up the mountain by cable car and then climb down. So we started early, before anyone was up, had a drink and some food at the hut on top of the mountain and then made our way to where the descent began. On this face of the mountain sheer walls and pinnacles fell to the screes far down below.

Max, with his serious sense of responsibility had brought felt climbing shoes, rope and a light bivouac tent. He attached me to the rope and then in his quiet way directed me where to place my foot and hand holds. I discovered that even on a precipitous slope I still had no fear of heights. Hold by hold I climbed down a wall the height of an average town house, looking between my legs to see where I was going.

After that there came a funnel which we came down leaning against one of its sides and pressing our feet against the other as we lowered ourselves inch by inch. Where there was solid rock I felt no fear. What caused me unease were worn paths parallel to the precipice where, although there was little danger, the footholds were loose and I was frightened of slipping.

About a third of the way down we were quite suddenly overtaken by a storm. Max took the bivouac tent from his pack. It had no tent poles but was the kind you sat on and pulled over your head. He had found a spot under a low wall of rock where we would be safe from falling stones. As we sat there right at the beginning of the storm, two young men in cotton shorts, tee shirts and plimsolls came up the gully beside us, laughing and shouting.

'Idiots,' said Max, 'a storm like this can loosen rocks and they could be killed.' They were too far away for any good advice, which in any case they surely would not have taken. Max was cross: 'It's fools like those who have accidents and make our parents worry about us. They think just because they are athletic they can do anything. They have no respect for the mountains.'

The rain thickened to hail and there were claps of thunder. Suddenly in the noise around us we heard something else. There were thuds of rocks bouncing down the gully and coming behind them we could hear something heavier. We held our breath as we both shared the same fear. But what came into sight, hurtling down the gully in enormous bounds was an uprooted tree trunk. It could well have been the body of a climber.

The storm passed and the sky was once more blue with harmless looking clouds, so we roped up again and continued on our way. It was now mainly down narrow paths right over the hanging precipices of the Rax. We could see the routes of far more advanced and dangerous climbs but we seemed to be alone on the mountain. At last we reached the high screes and Max told me that we must run down them. It was an exhilarating experience, like running in seven-league boots, for with each stride the screes on either side slipped down with us and it seemed as if the whole mountain side was sliding. We reached the bottom in a few minutes and walked back home along a stony road in the woods.

No-one asked where we had been, so our secret was kept. Max bought a postcard of the Rax and wrote on it a 'report' on my climbing. I came out of it fairly well and still have it somewhere amongst his letters.

In the late evenings and early mornings I wrote poetry in the privacy of my room. When I left I forgot to pack my folder of writings. This was the cause of the only cross letter I ever wrote to Max, for when he sent the poems on to me in Germany, he had read them. I was indignant that he should have looked at what I felt to be intensely private. He thought that as I was careless enough to leave them behind for him to post, he had a right to read them.

Only too quickly the weeks at Reichenau passed and Max put me on the train to Vienna. As he did not want to leave me till the last moment he came onto the train and we didn't notice when it was about to start. Along that bit of line it stopped at all the small local stations, so he was not carried back to Vienna with me. We laughed as we parted and he ran along the line waving until he was out of sight. I felt sadness at parting from him. I had no real wish to go back to England, where the university life that was planned for me seemed austere and without any connection with all the arts that Austria held for me. It did not occur to me that although my Austrian half was well in the ascendant, all my writing was in English and my English roots were strong too.

Back in Vienna, during the few days that remained, I was caught up in the preparations for going with Erich and Fine to their villa on the Isar some hours out of Munich. I packed all the books I had collected, mainly from the sorting out of Aunt Toni's library, in a large borrowed trunk. They included my great grandparents' collected Schiller, in an early nineteenth-century edition. My mother, after much nagging and begging on my part, had agreed to the expense. The rest was saying goodbye.

As we settled down in a third-class carriage for the night journey to Munich, the exhilaration of travelling towards new experiences balanced my sadness at parting from so many people I loved. For parting no longer seemed infinite as it had when I was a child, and we still had no notion of the danger that lay ahead. Erich and Fine had it in their minds that they might have to move from Germany, but Austria at any rate seemed safe.

I put my head on Fine's lap and slept. It was to be fifty years before I saw Vienna again.

13

THE KAHLERS' villa in Wolfratshausen had been redecorated and they decided that they could tidy it up better without my being about the place. They had arranged for me to stay for ten days in Munich with friends, a family called Meier.

Dr Meier was a Jew and a psychiatrist, his wife Elisabeth was the daughter of a Lutheran bishop. a very cultured woman and a pianist, though she had never aimed at being professional. There were four children and the elder two of these became my friends. Beate was a year older than me and Michael a year younger.

Beate and I spent long evenings talking over all our thoughts, discoveries and interests – the Meiers were part of the rich cultural life of Munich and knew many scholars and artists. I believe that Beate must have had some studies or other occupation during the day which I have now forgotten, for it seems looking back that it was always Michael who was my guide round the town. They had a house a short way from the centre and on a borrowed bicycle I followed him rather perilously, for I had had no experience of cycling in a capital. Crossing the wide squares where the traffic came pouring in disconcertingly from an unaccustomed side took some determination.

There were times when Mrs Meier took me round by myself and shared her delight in the churches, palaces and parks, and sometimes, I was sent to wander around alone. I became absorbed by this town so similar in many outward ways to Vienna and yet so different in spirit. Its cultural life was deep both in the past, in its galleries and history, and in the presence of many artists, poets and musicians who were living there at that time. But in spite of the modifying effect of the south on the harshness that was then showing itself in the rest of Germany, the very romanticism and traditionalism of Bavaria was nourishing the perverted patriotism of National Socialism.

The gentleness and good natured casualness of Vienna was absent. I had caught Munich at the last moment, when it was still possible to know and feel its pre-war flowering. The elections were imminent and the beerhalls crowded for speeches and rallies. I was taken to hear Brüning, the last liberal chancellor to win an election before Hitler came brutally to power. Perhaps it would have been historically more interesting to have heard Hitler, who was holding a meeting in a different beerhall. I was already becoming familiar with the raging red

banner headlines of *Der Stürmer*[12] and its obscene
vilification of the Jews. Even this sickening portent of
what was to come did not convince us. Beate and I and
her parents treated it with scorn and still clung to our
faith in that other Germany, the Germany of Goethe and
Bach, and other creative and sensitive people living or
dead.

We went on several excursions. One day we took a
train to visit friends who lived in the country. The little
station bore the name Dachau.[13] No shadow passed over
my mind as we walked along lanes to a house with a
large garden where we were welcomed by a small, lively
dark-haired woman who I found to my delight was the
stepdaughter of Josef Kainz, my hero of the Burgtheater.

The family proved to be very individual. There were
three sons living with their mother and they all had old-
German names. This later became a fashion with the
Nazis, but these people were far from National Socialism.
They were full of notions which were found among the
intelligentsia of that time. Their house was crowded with
books and musical instruments, and their garden with
vegetables and fruit – a sort of cultural market garden.
The younger Meier daughter was spending her holidays

---

[12] The most virulently antisemitic, pro Nazi newspaper of the time.
[13] At that time Dachau was best known for its colony of artists,
attracted by the local scenery. The concentration camp was not built
until 1933.

working there. I remember mainly a great deal of talk about art and the theatre – and the meal.

One of the precepts of the family was that there should be no servants and to achieve simplicity we had boards instead of plates and ate with our fingers, since the mother believed that with good manners you could eat as neatly with fingers only as with knives, forks and spoons. As we were eating salads, cold sliced meats and fruit, this was easy.

In Munich there was an exhibition of theatrical designs and photographs and I was overcome with a longing for the Burgtheater and resolved to ask my mother if I could go back to Vienna and perhaps study drama. I remembered the pleasure acting had given me at school and also had some idea of writing plays and intended to explain all this to her.

My stay in Munich passed quickly, Beate and I promised each other to keep in touch and I was put on a local train with wooden carriages and a toy-like engine which, puffing and rattling, took me up the valley of the Isar.

Wolfratshausen was a typical small Bavarian town, a lifesize version of the wooden toy houses and churches in small net bags which we had been given as presents. The Kahlers' villa was on slopes and terraces of the wide Isar valley. The house itself was on several levels and the gardens were shady, with little summer houses and wooden benches and tables where one could sit and gaze at the wonderful view of meadows, marshes and groups of trees, and villages with their onion crowned churches. On nights when the day had been particularly hot, a thick mist rose from the river and the moon shone down on a black and white Chinese landscape with only the knolls of the villages and the higher groups of trees rising above the mysterious whiteness.

Viele Grüsse von den Hunden in Wolfratshausen!

The garden had a very small oblong swimming pool deep enough to dive into but long enough only for about a dozen strokes. The house was full of books and modern paintings. A married couple looked after us and soon the many small bright guest rooms began to fill up.

The first to join us was Syl Aaron who appeared with his close friend Paula, a short, dark, robust young woman who worked on and off as an actress. They did not stay in the house but moved into a wooden building in the grounds. Paula was to help Fine with the housekeeping and Syl was to continue coaching me. As it turned out the house was soon so full and so many things were happening that there was not much time for work. The hours we snatched were spent on a bench in the woods, where I began Latin and read German classics to the croaking of small tree frogs in the branches.

The next to arrive were my mother and Pat. After a year at Uppingham he had developed a public school swagger and a variety of public school slang. In other ways he had hardly changed, but the gap between our ages seemed to have widened greatly.

Soon after my mother and Pat there came a friend of the Kahlers who stayed with them for the rest of the summer. Werner Gothein was an artist and owned a ceramic factory where he produced objects of his own design, with clean lines and clear colours. Strangely, his wife was not invited. The Kahlers found her dreary. She stayed in a hotel on the Starnberger See some hours away and Werner visited her very occasionally.

He was a gently confident man with quiet humour and the artist's concentration on and enjoyment of all the happy things in life. The weather during that idyllic summer was consistently fine and at night the stars sparkled brilliantly. Werner and I developed a great interest in the constellations and went out after dark with a star chart. Pat, of course, followed us and as Werner pointed out the more difficult signs and heavenly bodies he stood close behind me and leant his arm on my shoulder. Pat made the most of this and I discovered the disadvantage of having a younger brother following me about.

Erich, Werner, Pat and I would cycle to the Starnberger See. This romantic lake in which the mad King Ludwig had drowned was surrounded by woods and mountains and had a castle on its shores. We swam, ate delicious salmon trout and cycled back after dark, dangerously, for we had no lights and the road was steep and rough. The only way I could keep on it was to stare at the dim whiteness of Erich's shirt as he piloted us precariously home.

One day the Kahlers and some of their neighbours hired a vast wooden raft and with a boatman in charge we drifted down the Isar. We were a large and lively party of young and old and we swam and laughed and picnicked. Other friends picked us up at the end of the day and took us home.

Uncle Alfred and Aunt Mitzi came to stay and the Meiers travelled out from Munich to spend a day with us. In the visitors' book, large and legible, was the signature of D.H. Lawrence. His sister-in-law Else Jaffé had a house in the next village downstream and Frieda and Lawrence had been regular visitors of the Kahlers. The Jaffés were away from home so I did not have the chance of meeting Lawrence even at one remove.

Max Picard, philosopher and writer on art, came for some days with his son Michelchen. This boy, clumsy and rather babyish for his sixteen years, had been held up to me as a classical scholar. He was quiet and shy with a gentle smile. His mother had died when he was quite young and his father mothered and coddled him and seemed unaware that he was now a man. He did most things for his son, took all decisions and always had him sharing his bedroom. Max Picard was lively and interesting, but Michelchen sat about watching silently, a child with a man's intellect.

The long fine summer came to an end. We said our goodbyes and Werner came to see us off at the station in Munich. My mother, Pat and I had between us a sort of joking rivalry as to whom Werner was really coming to say farewell. For my mother, too, was charmed by him and Pat was child enough not to want to be outdone by me. When the moment came, the mystery was not solved, for he gave my mother a magazine, Pat a box of sweets and me a bunch of flowers.

Before going home to England we were to spend a week with Sasie in Lausanne. She was still in her ground floor flat on the shores of the lake. The surroundings were as lovely as ever but this short stay was darkened by sadness as I saw that Sasie, the person I loved most in the world, was now old. She walked slightly bowed and was tremulous and easily flustered. Perhaps it was rather that I was myself now a woman, but it was my first experience of someone who had been a strength in my life suddenly seeming to need my protection. It was very poignant and I spent hours of the night weeping.

I was also deeply saddened by a letter which came to me from Fine. She wrote long pages in which, for my own good, as she said, she accused me of being immature and full of futile and unrealistic enthusiasms. She cited my crushes on actors and poets who were dead. I was very hurt, not because I felt that she was right, but because she had so small an idea of the real nature of my feelings. I knew very well that my love and veneration of artists and writers was part of my engrossment in their work. It had never been a substitute for love and friendship with real people. I wrote a fervent letter defending myself, but our relationship was spoiled.

At this end of summer the lake was calm and beautiful in early morning mists, or in the evening sun which brought a gentle red to the rock and snow of the mountains. I had quite failed to persuade my mother to work out some future for me which would take me back to Vienna.

My life in England no longer seemed to belong to me, I had changed so much. Even my feelings for Tom seemed distant and unreal. I parted sorrowfully from Sasie as she saw us off on the late night train. The fear about the spirit of Germany which had been nourished by newspapers and the reading of Hitler's *Mein Kampf* was still balanced by hope, so I could not know that the riches of my Jewish and Austrian heritage that I carried away with me would never again be nourished at their source.

Love would keep me close to many of my family and friends scattered over the world, but that society, deeply artistic, cynical, humorous, contributing so much to music, medicine, law, journalism, philosophy, painting, drama and literature, where, young as I was, I had been accepted and shown kindness, and my particular corner of it, my dear family, would so soon have vanished from Vienna for ever.

14

S O I RETURNED to England, the country of my father. From then on, another distinct part of my life began. My work for the Oxford University entrance exams brought into my life the man I was to love and to marry. No-one could have been more essentially English. We settled in Cranleigh, where he was a master at the public school. My three children grew up entirely English. The Viennese Jewish girl that I had become during that precious last year in Vienna did not die away but grew within me and was often the cause both of conflict and of rich fulfilment.

The dangerous threat to my Austrian friends and relations waxed and waned and hung like a shadow over the joy of my courtship and marriage. After one last happy holiday in Aussee with my husband and baby daughter, the blow fell. Hitler marched into Austria.

Most of the people I knew closely escaped into some form of exile: Willy, already settled in the USA, was able to help many of his family and friends; Aunt Mitzi and Uncle Alfred, Lilly and her husband, Aunt Otti and Lily

Zingarelli, the twins Magda and Carla with their families
– all fled to the United States. Erich Kahler was offered a
post as professor at Princeton and he and Fine took Aunt
Toni to begin a new life there. Her interest in everything
around her was strong as ever and she lived into her
eighties, making many new friends, amongst whom the
closest was Albert Einstein. Richard Beer-Hofmann
arrived in the USA through Switzerland, in great sorrow
after the death of his beloved Paula. Dr Meier became
superintendant of a mental clinic on Long Island...

Others were scattered all over the earth – South
America, Israel, India are some of the countries where I
know my relations settled. Not all escaped. Uncle
Edmund, unable to face the terror approaching, shot
himself. Aunt Irene, joining friends in Poland, was heard
of no more. Aunt Jenny's son and his wife were caught
by the Nazis in their home in Brno, Georg Strakosch
committed suicide, Georg and Erich Steger's parents
went together to the gas chamber.

There were many who came to England. Max Perutz
was already in Cambridge working for a PhD and so was
able to bring his parents over to safety. My friendship with
him endured through the years and his son is my godson.
Max distinguishing himself by his research became head
of the Medical Research Council and a Nobel prizewinner.
His parents, like so many of their generation, were sad
refugees, too old to start a radically new life, living on in
material comfort but spiritual deprivation.

In the USA my first and second cousins married and had children and now there is a third generation of totally American young people, most of them unknown to me, but closely related.

So except as a potent memory, Vienna was lost to us all. After the war threads were picked up, visitors came, and with my mother and my husband and children I had one long summer holiday in Aussee. Here too there were reunions with those who had come over from their exile in America, Switzerland and elsewhere. The wall of the Trisselwand, the glacier of the Dachstein seemed eternal in their beauty and it was possible here to accept human comings and goings as incidental. I could not envisage Vienna without any of those people who were for me the very essence of its warmth and culture. I feared that it would remain haunted by Nazi brutality.

It has now come about that this recreating of my Viennese life, which had aroused great longing for the lovely town itself, and the persistence of my eldest granddaughter that she wanted to see Vienna, made me decide in the spring of this year, 1983, to return.

We flew in to the flat land to the south east and the airport coach took us through an area of motorways and factories with occasional small farmhouses where the blossom on the trees was just breaking. We were dropped at the Hilton Hotel, a replica of all Hilton Hotels the world over. Our next bus took us to the Stephansdom and carrying our light luggage we walked to our small hotel on the Petersplatz. The paved streets of this inner area are now cleared of traffic, which gives them an eighteenth century air. The cafés and hotels had moved chairs and tables out of doors and as there are no pavements, these streets which I had remembered as narrow looked spacious. To reach our small room in the hotel we had to walk along a pretty gallery over a courtyard, like the setting for a Mozart opera.

Almost immediately I felt at home, for Vienna in essence proved as changeless as the mountains. The old town beneath the Stephansdom's soaring steeple claimed me as it had before. Its legends are still alive. At the corner of the Kärntnerstrasse, the most fashionable shopping street, the tree trunk coated in iron by the apprentices' nails is still there behind its protecting rails. The basilisk lurks in its courtyard, and though now surrounded by blocks of flats, the gothic cross still marks the spot where, patiently spinning, a girl waited for her lover to return from the Crusade.

With Katie, my granddaughter, sixteen years old and fairheaded as I had been, I walked through the Belvedere, unchanged in its baroque loveliness, and saw the view of the Danube and the hills beyond. My memory had not failed me. We passed Uncle Alfred's house in the Jaurèsgasse, a few doors away from the dim little English Church, and followed my way to school down the Reisnerstrasse and through the Stadtpark, now rather less park and more recreation ground. The gardens of Schönbrunn and the Vienna Woods were miraculously filled with violets and birdsong. Once again I stood

before the Dürers in the Albertina and in the
Kunsthistorisches Museum. Here I found, aged as I was,
less pleasure in the Brueghels, which had once
transported me happily into the past, and far more in the
timeless portraits by Rembrandt and Velasquez.

Eating the ever delicious Viennese food, from the
coffee and fresh rolls brought to our bedroom in the
morning to Wienerschnitzel at night, sightseeing and
window shopping, everything linked me with the Vienna
I had known. These dear people who were no longer
there, who were exiled or dead, seemed now to be with
me. It was as if I contained them within myself, and I
could not help wondering how many of the vistors
around me – for it was the beginning of the tourist season
– were also making a pilgrimage to this city in order to
discover their roots. Young men and women with Jewish
faces might even be relatives of my own. I was experiencing
how in history the wounds of a town could heal.

There were two friends alone that we were able to
find. Gertrid Traxl, who had stayed with my daughter in
Guildford for an English language course, and visited me
in Devizes, welcomed us to her flat warmly. Her
hospitality represented for me the true Austrian character
with its humour, good nature and kindness. Everywhere
I was meeting it. A tragic and gruesome episode in
history could not be quite eliminated, but it had not
prevailed, and the young everywhere seemed untouched
and free of its taint.

It gave me joy to have a meeting with Lily Strakosch who had married Heinz Schnitzler and was a friend from past days. She had returned to live in Vienna from the United States, for her husband had longed once more to produce plays for the Viennese theatre, which was showing signs of a brilliant resurgence. They were able to reclaim their family house which I had known well, and Lily had brought her mother with them to end her days in Vienna. The years dropped away and I had no difficulty in finding in her the quiet, dark-eyed, gentle girl I had known. We talked of our children and grandchildren. She herself was devoted to music and was a violinist. One of her sons was now leader of an internationally famous string trio. Just before his recent death Heinz Schnitzler had brought out his father Arthur's diary and a volume of his letters. The soul of Vienna and its artistic life had proved indestructible.

There was one experience which came to me during this short visit which was as fresh and joyful as any I had had as a child. Katie has a great love of horses and so it was that we visited the Spanish Riding School. I had been inside the building in former days but never seen the horses, which may not have been in Vienna during the years that I was there.

We queued for one of the training periods, which lasted for a whole morning. The hall where this took place was like a huge rococo ballroom. Delicate as china figurines the horses were ridden and guided by men in uniforms of Maria Theresa's time. With priestlike concentration and patience they taught the horses steps and figures, very elegant and pure. As the ground was muffled by a thick layer of finely shredded leather, and instruction was given by gentle taps, movements of the body and tensions of the reins, it all passed in silence.

Of course what we longed for was to be able to watch a performance, but we knew that these were so fully booked that tickets had to be ordered many weeks beforehand. Nevertheless we decided to try; fortune was with us and we were offered two places.

It was evening, the chandeliers sparkled with light and music was playing. To Mozart, Beethoven, Weber and Strauss the horses performed their graceful and exact convolutions. Some of the 'airs' seemed to defy gravity, as when horses rose several feet above the ground with front and hind legs stretched out straight and seemed to remain poised for several seconds. The seventeenth-century coats and cocked hats of the riders underlined the military origin of all these movements, but there was no harshness. The whole performance had the poetry and joy of a ballet. After that performance a change affected my vision of Vienna and I saw what I had not seen before: in the parks and squares, in palace yards and on rooftops were stone horses, and riderless or ridden, they were one and all in poses that the beautiful Lipizzaner stallions had demonstrated to us.

The week drew to an end and we made our way to the Hilton to board our airport coach. There had not been time for all the things I would have loved to have done.

We had not visited modern galleries, browsed in bookshops, or been to the opera or theatre,

I hope very much that Katie felt that in some way she belonged to Vienna and was not a tourist like other tourists. I myself came back to my English home with a lively feeling that I had regained my heritage, and a freshly focussed love for all those individuals dead and living who are such an inalienable part of it.

Evelyn Louise Machin
Devizes, 1983

PICTURE INDEX

Front cover (L–R):   Pat, Charlie and Eve in Altaussee.

Back cover: Eve Machin in her sitting room in Devizes.

Lightning Source UK Ltd.
Milton Keynes UK
UKHW021017270721
387842UK00015B/1477

9 781914 938009